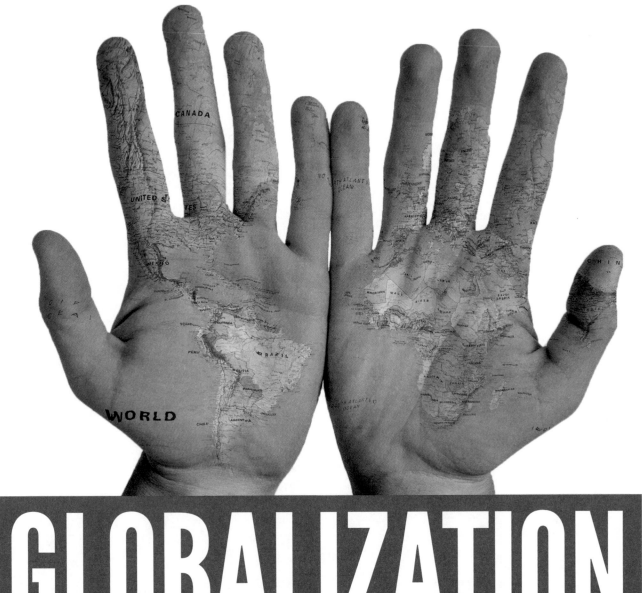

GLOBALIZATION
WHY WE CARE ABOUT FARAWAY EVENTS

Carla Mooney
Illustrated by Sam Carbaugh

Nomad Press
A division of Nomad Communications
10 9 8 7 6 5 4 3 2 1

This book was manufactured by Versa Press
East Peoria, Illinois
May 2018, Job # J17-12589

ISBN Softcover: 978-1-61930-666-0
ISBN Hardcover: 978-1-61930-664-6

Educational Consultant, Marla Conn

Questions regarding the ordering of this book should be addressed to
Nomad Press
2456 Christian St.
White River Junction, VT 05001
www.nomadpress.net

Printed in the United States.

Titles in the Inquire & Investigate
Great Events of the Twentieth Century set

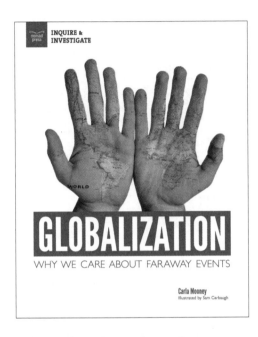

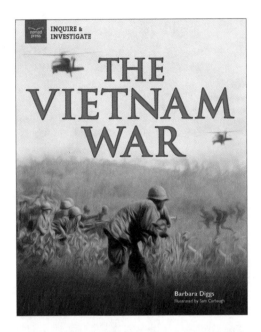

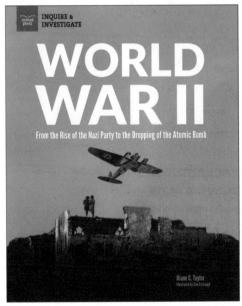

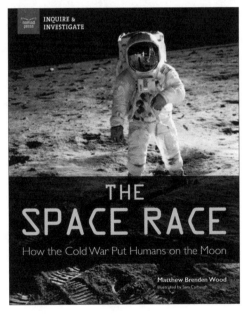

Interested in primary sources? **Look for this icon.**

You can use a smartphone or tablet app to scan the QR codes and explore more! Cover up neighboring QR codes to make sure you're scanning the right one. You can find a list of URLs on the Resources page.

If the QR code doesn't work, try searching the internet with the Keyword Prompts to find other helpful sources.

 Globalization

What are source notes?

In this book, you'll find small numbers at the end of some paragraphs. These numbers indicate that you can find source notes for that section in the back of the book. Source notes tell readers where the writer got their information. This might be a news article, a book, or another kind of media. Source notes are a way to know that what you are reading is true information that other people have verified. They can also lead you to more places where you can explore a topic that you're curious about!

Contents

TIMELINE

Around 550 BCE ..... The Greek philosopher Anaximander creates what is believed to be the first world map.

100s BCE .... The Silk Road trade route across Central Asia connects China and Europe.

1864 CE .... The first Geneva Convention is adopted to protect sick and wounded military personnel, regardless of nationality.

1892 .... Coca-Cola is founded.

1930 .... The U.S. Congress passes the Smoot-Hawley Tariff Act to protect workers and industries by raising tariffs on imported goods by nearly 60 percent. In response, countries around the world also raise tariffs on imported goods.

1944 .... The World Bank is established.

1945 .... World War II ends, opening the door to more trade between nations.

1945 .... The United Nations (UN) is founded.

1945 .... The UN Charter establishes the International Court of Justice, which hears disputes between nations in matters of international law.

1947 .... The General Agreement on Trade and Tariffs (GATT) is signed to negotiate trade rules.

1948 .... The United Nations adopts the Universal Declaration of Human Rights, which lists the fundamental human rights that are to be universally protected.

1952 .... Belgium, Germany, France, Italy, Luxembourg, and the Netherlands form the European Coal and Steel Community.

1962 .... The first Walmart store opens in Arkansas.

1967 .... The first international McDonald's fast food restaurants open in Canada and Puerto Rico.

1970 .... The Nuclear Non-Proliferation Treaty goes into effect, aiming to prevent the global spread of nuclear weapons and weapons technology.

1975 .... Advances in computers, satellites, and electronics increase global trade.

1984 .... British musicians organize a charity event to benefit starving Ethiopian people in response to a documentary about famine in Ethiopia.

1991 .... The World Wide Web is launched, making global communication quicker and easier.

1993 .... The European Union is established, increasing economic, political, and social ties among European nations.

1994 .... Signed by the United States, Canada, and Mexico, the North American Free Trade Agreement (NAFTA) comes into force.

1995 .... The World Trade Organization is established in Geneva, Switzerland.

1999 .... The European Union introduces the euro to world financial markets.

2002 .... The Rome Statute comes into force and establishes the International Criminal Court.

2006 .... The UN establishes the Human Rights Council, which works to promote and protect human rights worldwide.

2007 .... The Great Recession begins in the United States and quickly spreads to economies around the world.

2012 .... The International Criminal Court convicts Thomas Lubanga, the leader of a militia in the Democratic Republic of Congo, of war crimes.

2013 .... China overtakes the United States to become the world's largest trading nation.

2014 .... Soccer's World Cup is shown in every country and territory in the world to an audience of more than 3.2 billion people.

2015 .... More than 1 million migrants and refugees flood Europe, prompting several European nations to put measures in place to limit immigration.

2015 .... The UN adopts the Paris Agreement to address climate change.

2016 .... The United Kingdom voters pass a referendum to begin the process of withdrawing from the European Union.

2017 .... More than 36,000 McDonald's fast food restaurants around the world serve Big Macs and French fries to millions of people every day.

2017 .... People around the world rally to donate money and supplies and volunteer for relief efforts to aid victims of Hurricane Irma in the Caribbean.

Introduction ▷
The World Cup on a Global Stage

RIO 2014, A GLOBAL BALL!

How does the FIFA World Cup represent globalization?

The coming together of many different nationalities from all around the world at the 2014 FIFA World Cup in Brazil is indicative of the daily merging of our global experiences, from eating bananas grown in Guatemala to riding bikes made in China.

• • • • • • • • • • • •

In July 2014, people from all around the globe gathered in Brazil for one of the world's most popular sporting events—the men's football World Cup. Organized by the International Federation of Association Football (FIFA), the World Cup is held every four years. It has been hosted by countries on every continent except Australia and Antarctica.

For the 2014 event, 32 of the world's best national teams competed to win the Golden Globe Trophy. These teams included five from Africa, four from Asia, 13 from Europe, four from North and Central America, and six from South America.

Not only were the teams themselves from around the world, so were the fans. More than a million international tourists traveled to Brazil from countries as far away as Germany, Australia, Japan, and Israel. They dressed in team colors and waved the flags of their nations as they cheered for their favorite teams.

An even larger global audience watched the sporting action on television and on digital streaming devices. The 2014 World Cup was shown in every country and territory in the world to an audience of more than 3.2 billion people. Multinational corporations such as Adidas, Coca-Cola, Visa, Emirates, McDonald's, Sony, and Hyundai Motor Group poured money into the event for sponsorships. Their brands and logos were seen daily by the billions of viewers.

The official slogan of the 2014 FIFA World Cup was *Juntos num so ritmo*, or "All in one rhythm." It truly was a global event.

A PRODUCT OF GLOBAL COOPERATION

Adidas, a German corporation, supplied the soccer balls used in the World Cup. More than a million Brazilian fans voted in a social media contest, naming the ball "Brazuca."

The ball itself was a product of global cooperation. Low-wage workers in Pakistan made the balls used in game play, while Chinese workers manufactured replica balls. The manufacturing process used chemical compounds from several countries and plastics made from petroleum from the Middle East and Norway.

More than 600 international soccer players from all positions tested prototypes of the Brazuca balls to make sure they worked properly. They conducted tests in 10 countries on three continents, in different climates and altitudes.

PRIMARY SOURCES

Primary sources come from people who were eyewitnesses to events. They might write about the event, take pictures, post short messages to social media or blogs, or record the event for radio or video. The photographs in this book are primary sources, taken at the time of the event. Paintings of events are usually not primary sources, since they were often painted long after the event took place. What other primary sources can you find? Why are primary sources important? Do you learn differently from primary sources than from secondary sources, which come from people who did not directly experience the event?

credit: Danilo Borges

Once the balls were ready, South-Korean-built container ships carried the Brazucas to fans around the globe.

Even the World Cup's entertainment was a product of global cooperation. At the opening ceremony, American entertainer Jennifer Lopez took center stage at the Arena de Sao Paulo. Dressed in a flashy green playsuit, Lopez was joined by American rapper Pitbull and Brazilian singer Claudia Leitte to sing Brazil 2014's official song, "We are One (Ole Ola)."

The original song was a global collaboration. The three performers, along with six other musical artists from three continents, co-wrote the song together. The song became a commercial success and reached the top 20 on *Billboard* music charts in 27 countries.

The song's message reaches out to people around the world to come together as one to tackle serious global problems.

Soon after the song's release, Pitbull spoke about his happiness at being involved in the project. "I'm honored to join Jennifer Lopez and Claudia Leitte at the FIFA World Cup to bring the world together," said Pitbull. "I truly believe that this great game and the power of music will help unify us, because we are best when we are one."[1]

GLOBAL CONNECTIONS

As the FIFA World Cup demonstrates, people around the world are becoming increasingly connected, doing business, exchanging money, and sharing ideas and culture. You can see these connections in your own life.

At the supermarket, you can buy food from all over the world—olive oil from Greece, bananas from Guatemala, and coffee from South America. At home, you surf the internet on a computer made in Asia, reading news from all over the world. Your parents might drive an American-, Japanese-, or German-made car, while you listen to music from American and Canadian pop stars. And in school and in the community, you have friends who have moved here from other countries.

Around the world, people from different societies and cultures have made contact throughout the centuries, exchanging goods and ideas. In recent years, the pace of that exchange has increased tremendously.

TRUE NEWS

The 2014 FIFA World Cup welcomed a new country, with the team from Bosnia-Herzegovina playing in its first major tournament.

WE ARE ONE

You can listen to the official song of the 2014 FIFA World Cup at this website. Do the lyrics present globalization as a positive or negative thing? How can you tell? Why might this song be attractive to people of many different nationalities?

🔍 We Are One (Ole Ola)

How many independent countries are in the world? It seems like a simple question, but the answer is actually a bit complicated. Depending on who you ask, the answer can range from 189 to 201. According to the United Nations (UN), there are 195 sovereign states around the world. A sovereign state is a place with its own borders and completely independent government. To get to 195, the UN counts its 193 member states plus the two UN Observer States of Vatican City and Palestine.[2] There are six states that are not counted by the UN. These states are claimed as parts of other countries, but are not completely controlled by them. Although not recognized by the UN, these states may be recognized by some UN members as separate countries.[3]

Advances in transportation and technology have made it easier than ever to connect with people on the other side of the world. Jet airplanes and great ocean ships carry people and goods everywhere. Cell phones, computers, the internet, and social media allow people to communicate instantly, no matter where they are.

Through globalization, the world is becoming more interconnected and interdependent. Money, technology, raw materials, and finished goods move quickly across borders.

> Global connections also encourage the flow of ideas and cultures among communities.

As a result, economies, laws, and social movements are forming at the international level. Instead of living isolated lives in our own communities, we are more connected and reliant on each other than ever before. We are becoming a global community.

Not everyone thinks this is a good thing. There is a debate about whether globalization is beneficial for all people. Some people believe that globalization favors the wealthy and educated. Smaller companies and poorer countries are at risk of being left behind, unable to compete in a connected world. And many fear that local cultures, languages, and traditions are being lost through globalization.

What do you think? Is an interconnected world a better place to live or are we losing vital parts of our identities when we all have access to the same things?

Globalization: Why We Care About Faraway Events examines globalization, focusing on how it is defined, how technology is driving it, and how it is affecting economies, political systems, laws, human rights, and cultures around the world. This book also explores the future of globalization and some of the issues the global community will face in coming years.

The text and activities will encourage you to think critically and creatively about how globalization affects local and global communities. By understanding the history and factors that drive globalization, you will gain a better understanding of the benefits and costs to people around the world.

How are you going to contribute to our global neighborhood?

VOCAB LAB

Write down what you think each word means. What root words can you find to help you? What does the context of the word tell you?

brand, **collaboration**, **culture**, **economy**, **global**, **interconnected**, **international**, **multinational nationality**, **prototype**, and **technology**.

Compare your definitions with those of your friends or classmates. Did you all come up with the same meanings? Turn to the text and glossary if you need help.

KEY QUESTIONS

- **How does the World Cup reflect the idea of globalization? Can you think of other events that many countries take part in together?**

- **How does technology contribute to the increased speed of connections around the world?**

- **What do you think someone from the early 1900s would think about how we trade, travel, and communicate today?**

WHO MAKES IT?

Supporters of globalization promise that global trade will expand the wealth of countries by lowering the price of goods, increasing worker wages, and increasing economic growth. In this activity, you will investigate where the products you use come from and evaluate the impact of global trade on these countries.

- **To begin, select 10 items that you own.** Look at each item's label to determine where it was made. Have several other classmates, family, or friends each select 10 items to research as well.

- **Where does each product come from?** Create a list of countries. What trends do you notice? Which countries produced the most goods on your list?

- **Next, investigate the minimum wage in each country and the gross domestic product (GDP) of each country.** Create a chart that displays the information you have researched.

- **Looking at your chart, think about the following questions.**

  - What trends do you notice, if any?

  - Which countries produce the most goods that you buy?

  - Which countries produce the least amount of goods that you buy?

  - How do the wages and GDP compare for countries that produce more goods vs. countries that produce less goods?

  - How do wages and GDP compare for these countries to the United States?

To investigate more, create a map to show the countries where the products you buy are made. What patterns do you notice on the map? Select three countries and investigate their main exports. Does each country specialize in a particular type of product to export? Why or why not?

Chapter 1 ▷
What Is Globalization?

WOW... IT SEEMS LIKE EVERYTHING COMES FROM ALL OVER THE WORLD!

Why is globalization happening at a faster rate today?

Many different factors contribute to the increased rate of globalization, including ease of travel, eased trade regulations, and improved communications technology.

* * * * * * * * * * * * *

Today, you can wear clothes made in Asia, eat Mexican food at a local restaurant, and watch a movie made in Italy, all while living in the United States. Centuries ago, that would not have been possible. Globalization allows you to live in a world with many connections to other countries and cultures. But what exactly does that mean? And how does globalization affect people around the world?

In its simplest form, globalization is a process of integrating communication, culture, and economies all around the world into a global system. Countries no longer operate as independent islands. Instead, people, companies, and governments of different nations work together.

Goods, services, people, culture, and ideas flow across borders throughout the world. As a result, the world is more closely connected. In a way, it is becoming a much smaller place.

Advances in technology mean that people are no longer restricted by national borders or distance. New communications technology, such as cell phones and the internet, allow people to instantly communicate and do business with people on the other side of the globe. They can use cell phones, fax machines, email, text messaging, and social media to communicate.

Jet airplanes fly people around the world in less than 24 hours. Planes, vehicles, and ships carry goods and services more easily across borders. Because of these advances, the exchange of ideas and goods over vast distances has become more common and faster than ever.

GLOBALIZATION IN HISTORY

Globalization is not new—it has happened throughout history. Globalization occurred when people traveled from one nation to another and exchanged goods, ideas, and culture. More than 2,000 years ago, Alexander the Great was the king of the ancient Greek kingdom of Macedon. As he conquered new lands, his armies spread ancient Greek culture to many places in southwestern Asia, northern Africa, and southern Europe.

During the Middle Ages, the famous Silk Road stretched across Central Asia and connected China and Europe. The trading route passed the northern borders of China, India, and Persia (now Iran) to Eastern Europe, near modern-day Turkey and the Mediterranean Sea. Merchants and tradesmen traveled in large caravans along the route. They carried silk cloth, tea, salt, sugar, porcelain, and spices from China and the East. In Europe, they exchanged these items for goods such as cotton, ivory, wool, gold, and silver.

The Trans-Saharan Trade Route played an important role in spreading the religion of Islam.

• • • • • • • • • • • •

The Silk Road generated trade among several kingdoms and empires. Along with the exchange of goods, it also provided a way for ideas, culture, knowledge, technology, art, and religion to spread across the settled world. Many trading centers along the route, including Aleppo, in modern-day Syria, and Mosul, in modern-day Iraq, became important cultural centers.

In Africa, the Trans-Saharan Trade Route linked North Africa to West Africa. A number of paths spread across the Sahara Desert, first appearing in the fourth century CE. Caravans with more than a thousand camels carried goods such as gold, salt, cloth, and slaves.

Arabic knowledge, education, and language, expanded from the Berber people in North Africa to people living in West Africa. When European countries established colonies in Australia, Africa, North America, and South America, they exchanged goods, ideas, and culture with the native peoples they encountered.

The Silk Road

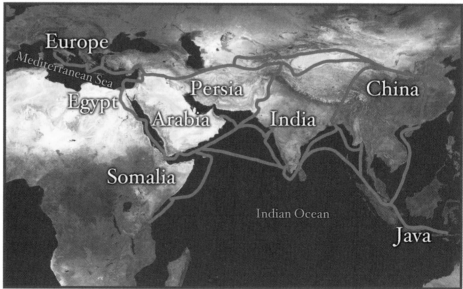

In recent years, the pace and scope of globalization has increased. There are many reasons for this, including an increase in the number of people, countries, and industries. The pace of globalization had been limited by two factors: transportation and technology. Most people remained in their birth town or village for their entire lives. Globalization was a slow process.

SPEEDING UP

While globalization has existed for centuries, the pace of it quickened in the nineteenth century. During this time, world trade increased in what is called the "first wave of globalization." Technological advances such as factory machines, steam engines, combustion engines, and railroads reduced manufacturing and trade costs, allowing companies to sell their products faster and farther afield. International trade grew steadily every year until World War I.

Between World War I and World War II, the Great Depression hit the United States and the rest of the world. Globalization slowed as several countries passed measures to restrict free trade in order to improve their own economies.

After World War II, international trade increased again. Improvements in communications and transportation made it possible for companies to more easily expand their operations into foreign countries. Transnational corporations emerged. These corporations have a base or headquarters in one country, but have operations in several other countries. During the late twentieth century and early twenty-first century, the rate of globalization has increased tremendously. Since 1950, the volume of world trade has increased 20 times.

Travel across great distances was long and hard in the past. Only a limited number of people, such as merchants and adventurers, made these kinds of journeys before modern transportation.

· · · · · · · · · · · · ·

SHRINKING BARRIERS TO TRADE

What has caused globalization to speed up so quickly? One explanation is the reduction in barriers to trade. In the years since World War II, many governments have removed barriers that regulated trade between countries and embraced free-market economic systems.

In a free market, the prices of goods and services are determined by supply and demand, or by how much someone is willing to pay for something. This changes according to how hard that thing is to get. Neither the government nor any other organization interferes with restrictions, regulations, or price-setting.

In addition, governments created international agreements to promote trade. They negotiated with other governments to further reduce barriers to international trade. In this trade-friendly environment, companies are able to increase their own production of goods and services. Governments have also taken advantage of new opportunities in foreign countries. They have built foreign factories, raised capital from foreign investors, and distributed and sold more products to customers worldwide.

WHAT ABOUT TECHNOLOGY?

Advances in technology have helped to connect the world and speed up the pace of globalization. In recent years, computers, cell phones, and mobile devices have become smaller, more efficient, and more affordable. They have changed the way we live.

Imagine what life was like before cell phones, computers, and the internet. How would you talk to someone who lived far away from you? You'd probably have to write a letter, then wait for a reply.

Today, you can use a cell phone to call anyone around the world and talk to them instantly. If they are not available, you can leave a voice mail or send a text message.

It wasn't always like this! Until the mid-1950s, communication across the Atlantic and Pacific Oceans was slow and difficult. Commercial telephone service using high-frequency radio opened between London, England, and New York in 1927. This radio telephone service was noisy, unreliable, and very expensive. It cost $75 for the first three minutes of a phone call![1]

In 1956, American Telephone and Telegraph Co. (AT&T) introduced the first transatlantic telephone cable, called TAT-1. The cable could carry 36 calls at a time at a cost of $12 per call for the first three minutes. The TAT-1 cable produced higher-quality service, more capacity, better-quality phone calls, and greater security. The number of transatlantic telephone calls skyrocketed, from about 10,000 in 1927 to more than 4 million in 1961. Soon, large corporations used the telephone cable to communicate and coordinate overseas operations.

"HELLO?"

You can listen to the first telephone call across the transatlantic telephone cable, between New York, Ottawa, Canada, and London, at this website. What must it have felt like to talk with people on the other side of the ocean for the first time?

🔍 TAT-1 mp3

Engineers at AT&T make plans to run a cable across the Atlantic Ocean in 1922.

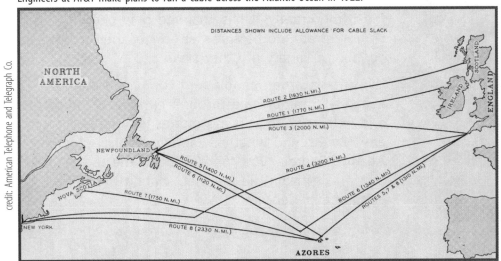

credit: American Telephone and Telegraph Co.

DISTANCES SHOWN INCLUDE ALLOWANCE FOR CABLE SLACK

NORTH AMERICA

ROUTE 2 (1930 N. MI.)
ROUTE 1 (1770 N. MI.)
ROUTE 3 (2000 N. MI.)
NEWFOUNDLAND
ROUTE 5 (1400 N. MI.)
ROUTE 6 (1120 N. MI.)
ROUTE 4 (3200 N. MI.)
NOVA SCOTIA
ROUTE 7 (1750 N. MI.)
ROUTE 6 (1340 N. MI.)
ROUTES 5, 7 & 8 (1310 N. MI.)
NEW YORK
ROUTE 8 (2330 N. MI.)
IRELAND
SCOTLAND
ENGLAND
AZORES

While telephone cables opened up communication for many, large areas of the world were still not connected. Beginning in the 1980s, satellite communication systems opened up communication to remote locations, including the edges of Antarctica and Greenland.

INVENTING THE INTERNET

A key driver of globalization, the internet evolved through the efforts of several government agencies and university scientists. It was initially developed to ease communications between computers at universities. The internet provided a way for computers on different networks to communicate with one another. As the internet grew, it connected millions of computers around the world and formed a communication network.

> The internet has revolutionized how people are connected worldwide.

It provides a common platform where people and businesses can communicate and share information. Most importantly, it has changed how people communicate, do business, shop, get their news, and conduct a variety of other tasks.

With the internet, people and companies can instantly communicate through email, chat programs, and video phone calls, no matter how far away they are located. And whether you live Beijing, China, or Atlanta, Georgia, you can download the same music and movies from the internet, sharing the same cultural experience.

Images from the 2004 tsunami in Thailand could be seen around the world almost immediately after the event.

credit: David Rydevik

The internet has also changed the way people get the news. In earlier decades, most people only had access to news from local networks and a few national networks in their own country. Only a few companies, such as CNN, broadcast in multiple countries. Today, global media networks bring news and information about current events to people worldwide. On the internet, people can read about events in Russia and Pakistan. They can see live footage of a natural disaster in Peru or a terrorist attack in London.

It's not just facts that are so much easier to access now. People are also able to read and see the news from different perspectives and discover what people in other countries consider important. It might not be what people in their own country find interesting!

Even people who do not know each other can connect and make new friends through online communities and social networking sites.

● ● ● ● ● ● ● ● ● ● ●

ZOOM AROUND THE WORLD

If you were going to travel to another country 100 years ago, how would you go? How long would it take? Much longer than it does now! Advances in technology have improved transportation, making it easier for people and goods to travel by road, rail, sea, and air. In all these modes of transportation, vehicles have become larger, faster, cheaper to operate, and more environmentally friendly.

The use of computer technology, as well as innovations in satellite navigation and the global positioning system (GPS), have made operating these vehicles easier and more efficient, too.

On the road, cars are faster, safer, and more fuel-efficient. They are cheaper to operate and less expensive to buy. These improvements allow more people to travel greater distances.

This plane can fly straight from London to Singapore without stopping.

credit: Adrian Pingstone

In the air, jet airplanes have expanded the tourism industry and trade across countries and continents. Passenger planes have become cheaper and faster, allowing more people to travel and experience different countries and cultures. In 1934, a flight from London to Singapore took eight days to complete, with 22 layovers to refuel. That means the plane had to stop in places such as Athens, Gaza, Baghdad, Calcutta, and Bangkok to refill the gas tank! Today, that same flight takes only 12 hours.

Advances in ships and railroads have also changed the way companies do business. Supertankers are massive container ships that can carry enormous quantities of goods. Using supertankers, companies can ship more goods to customers in other countries. As a result, international trade has increased.

THE DARK SIDE

Some people oppose globalization. While globalization does a lot of good, it also can be harmful. Some people argue that an international free market has benefitted only multinational corporations in the West, while harming local companies, cultures, and poorer people.

One claim is that globalization widens the gap between the wealthy and the poor. While citizens who belong to wealthier countries, such as the United States, benefit the most from globalization, poor people and citizens from developing nations are at a disadvantage. They are sometimes exploited as cheap labor for international corporations. Many people in developing countries do not have access to technology or speak English, an increasingly important language in the global world.

GLOBAL ECONOMY

Many poorer nations have struggled to compete in a global economy. The citizens of these countries are less likely to be educated or have the skills to improve their economies. The citizens who are skilled and educated often move to more developed countries to enjoy a better standard of living. This leaves the undeveloped country to struggle without the skilled workers it needs to improve its economy.

In the year 2000, emerging economies accounted for 12 percent of global wealth, but by 2016 had contributed nearly 25 percent toward global growth.[3]

- How do you think human behavior has changed since the rate of globalization has sped up during the past century?

- Do you think it's a good thing that businesses such as McDonald's and KFC can be found all around the world? Would you visit one of those businesses if you were traveling in a foreign country? Why or why not?

Globalization has also created more transnational corporations (TNCs) that do business in multiple countries. TNCs that use cheap foreign labor can sell goods and services at lower prices. As a result, many smaller, local companies, which must pay higher prices for labor and raw materials, cannot compete and are being forced out of business.

In response, some industries have started campaigns to promote local markets and locally produced goods and services. Have you heard the phrase, "buy local?"

Pop culture from the United States and other Western countries has replaced local customs and traditions in some places. Cities around the world have Western fast food chains, such as McDonald's or Kentucky Fried Chicken (KFC). As English has become the dominant global language, many smaller local languages are being lost.

In many countries, traditional clothing is being replaced by Western clothing.

Globalization can be a positive force around the world, promoting economic growth, prosperity, and democratic freedom. Yet for billions of people, globalization threatens their livelihoods and cultures and is changing traditional ways of life.

Citizens of all countries are affected by globalization. The choices we make now will shape how globalization develops in the years to come. By understanding how globalization works, along with the issues and controversies related to it, we can find the right balance of globalization to improve life for all people on Earth.

SHOW THE CONNECTIONS

Globalization is the great connector, bringing together people, ideas, and more from all around the world. You can learn about these connections simply by studying something from your everyday life. Pick three items that you use on a daily basis. They could be music you listen to, a T-shirt you wear, the bed you sleep in, the toothpaste you use, or the apple you eat.

VOCAB LAB

Write down what you think each word means. What root words can you find to help you? What does the context of the word tell you?

caravan, **controversy**, **copyright**, **exploit**, **free market**, **globalization**, **tariffs**, **trade barrier**, **trade prosperity**, and **transnational corporation**.

Compare your definitions with those of your friends or classmates. Did you all come up with the same meanings? Turn to the text and glossary if you need help.

- **For each item, think about the following.**

  - Is your item affected by globalization?

  - Where is it made or grown?

  - Where is it shipped to?

  - How is it transported?

  - What laws affect it?

  - Who benefits from it and why?

  - Who suffers from it and why?

- **Create a map on poster board or in PowerPoint to illustrate the global connections you have found for each object.** Present the map and findings to your class.

- **How are the journey and connections for each item similar?**

- **How are they different?**

> **To investigate more,** pick a country to research. Write an essay on how globalization has impacted the country, both positively and negatively.

Chapter 2 ▶
Money in a Global World

BUT WAIT... HOW DO PEOPLE PAY FOR GOODS FROM ALL AROUND THE WORLD? JUST TRADING?

What does trade look like in a global setting?

Countries trade with other countries to make it possible for people to get the goods they need. Efficiency is one main goal, and making a profit is another.

• • • • • • • • • • • • •

Many years ago, people lived in small groups. They grew and hunted their own food, made their own clothes, and built their own homes and goods. The materials they used and the goods they produced often depended on where they lived. A group living near the ocean caught a lot of their food by fishing, while a group living near forests trapped and hunted animals for food and used pelts to make clothing and blankets.

Members of a group often became skilled at producing cloth, tools, or other items that another group might not have. As groups traveled and interacted with their neighbors, they came in contact with even more groups. They discovered that some communities were able to grow different crops or make different tools and clothing. People who had lived near the ocean and eaten mainly fish might have been amazed at the taste of venison from the deer hunted by people who lived in the forest.

Have you ever tried food from a different location or culture? What kind of experience was it?

Through trade, each group could enjoy what the other produced. Every group had access to more products. People gained more knowledge. They learned how other groups made goods or grew crops. No longer did they have to produce everything they needed themselves. Instead, they could create whatever they were skilled at making and trade for other goods they needed. How do you think this changed individual lives?

As transportation improved, people traveled farther and faster. Ships sailed around the globe, so more opportunities to trade arose. As travel became easier and easier to accomplish, the distance between the people who produced goods and those who purchased them increased more and more.

WHAT IS GLOBAL TRADE?

In its simplest form, trade is buying and selling goods or services. One person sells something that another person buys. You might make a T-shirt that you sell to your neighbor across the street. That's trade! Now, what if you sold a T-shirt to a person in Argentina? That's global trade.

Global trade occurs when one person sells something that another person in a different country buys. Another way to say this is one country exports (sells) goods that another country imports (buys).

TRUE NEWS

Before money came into use, people exchanged goods and services through bartering. Bartering is an agreement to trade a certain quantity of a good or service in exchange for another good or service. In this system, the bartered goods have the same estimated value.

Sometimes, people export goods because they can produce a product at a cost that allows them to compete on a global stage. For example, some countries are able to easily produce large amounts of agricultural products, such as coffee in Columbia or cocoa in Cote d'Ivoire. Other countries have large amounts of natural resources, such as oil or iron ore. These countries export their goods to other countries that need them.

Countries also export goods because they might be able to charge higher prices abroad than they can at home. People in wealthier nations can spend more money on goods such as food and clothing, while people in developing nations don't have the money to spend on what they consider luxuries. What are some things you buy that a kid in a developing nation couldn't afford?

Why do people import goods?

In some cases, they might not have the items in their home country. People in Pennsylvania cannot grow bananas or coffee beans in their backyards. To get these goods, they buy bananas from Ecuador and coffee from Brazil.

Countries might import goods because another country makes better or cheaper products. China is one of the world's leading electronic equipment manufacturers. A company in China might be able to make and export electronics much more cheaply than a U.S. company can make them. As a result, the Chinese company can sell at a lower price.

People in the United States buy Chinese electronics because they are less expensive. Do you have a smart phone or a tablet? How much did it cost? Where was it made?

The Volkswagen Beetle is a German-made car that is very popular in the United States.

Today, container ships transport goods around the world.

credit: NOAA

Countries also import essential goods that they cannot produce enough of themselves to meet their needs at a reasonable price. Oil is an essential good in the United States. In 2016, the country imported approximately 10.1 million barrels of petroleum per day from about 70 countries, according to the U.S. Energy Information Administration.[1]

DISCONTINUED

The United States has almost entirely stopped producing some goods because foreign producers can make these goods faster, more cheaply, and often better. Many types of clothing can be manufactured more cheaply in foreign countries, such as China and India, because they have a lower cost of labor. In fact, the United States imports nearly all of its clothes, 97.5 percent according to the American Apparel & Footwear Association. The United States has also stopped making some electronic equipment, because foreign competitors can make them more efficiently.

TRUE NEWS

In 2016, China was the top textile exporter.

CHEAP OIL

The United States could stop importing foreign oil and rely solely on oil produced in America. However, the costs of producing the extra oil or using alternative energy sources—such as coal, nuclear power, or hydro-electric power—would be more expensive for consumers. Therefore, the United States continues to import reasonably priced foreign oil to meet its energy needs. It's the least-expensive option.

TRADE SPECIALIZATION

The cost of producing goods varies by country. It might cost $10 to build a chair in one country and $12 to build the same chair in another country. Production costs vary because of several key factors in the production process—labor, equipment and technology, land, and natural resources. These differences influence which goods countries import and export.

Some countries, especially in developing areas of the world, have many low-skill workers who are willing to work for lower wages. Goods that require a lot of low-skill labor can be produced more cheaply in these countries.

> Where was your shirt made? It's likely that it was manufactured in a country that has many low-skill laborers.

In contrast, the production of some goods requires expensive equipment and technology, also known as capital. In developing countries, capital is scarce and expensive. In wealthy countries such as the United States, capital is more common and less expensive. Therefore, it makes sense for companies in the United States to produce goods that require a lot of capital. The top exports of the United States include commercial aircraft, industrial machines, semiconductors, chemicals, and petroleum products.[2]

Countries usually benefit by specializing in producing goods that their available labor, capital, land, and resources allow them to produce most efficiently and cheaply. They trade these goods for products made in other countries.

Exports help the United States and other industrialized countries maintain high levels of employment. Lots of workers are needed to produce the goods that are exported.

● ● ● ● ● ● ● ● ● ● ● ●

To learn more about trade specialization, check out this Crash Course video. How does global trade make lives better in the countries that trade? What are some of the problems with international trade?

 Crash Course economics #2

The Boeing Everett Plant in Everett, Washington, where the company assembles wide-body Boeing airplanes

credit: Maurice King

In some cases, a country might be better than other countries at producing all of the products they are able to manufacture. For example, U.S. companies might be able to produce both tables and computers more efficiently and cheaply than foreign competitors. However, instead of making both, the U.S. companies will often specialize in producing computers, which they can make with the greatest efficiency and cost advantages. This is called the theory of comparative advantage.

According to the theory, all countries benefit from trading with one another regardless of how efficiently they can produce any one type of good. When countries specialize in the products in which they have the greatest efficiencies and cost advantages, everyone benefits. Everyone can buy one another's best products.

DRAWBACKS

In most cases, trade specialization benefits everyone involved. Yet, in some situations, trade specialization can have negative consequences. When a country or region focuses on producing a particular product or good, there is a risk that resources will be over-exploited in order to increase production. For example, a region that produces lumber may cut down more trees in order to increase sales. Cutting down too many trees can damage the environment and exhaust the resource. In addition, trade specialization can lead to structural unemployment. When a region specializes in producing certain goods or services, jobs for workers in other industries can decline.

In reality, trade specialization does not always work the way the theory of comparative advantage would predict. In the real world, no country specializes in the production of only a single product! Also, all countries produce some goods that another country could produce more efficiently. Italy might be able to produce shoes more efficiently than Mexico. Yet if Italian shoe makers cannot find Mexican buyers or cannot transport the shoes cheaply to Mexico, they might not sell the shoes in Mexico. In this case, Mexican companies would continue to make shoes locally.

SUPPLY AND DEMAND

Imagine it's a hot day and a team of construction workers is laying the foundation for the new middle school in your town. You know the workers are going to be thirsty, so you bring 30 cups of lemonade to sell for $1 each. But there are 60 construction workers. There's not enough lemonade to go around. Are you tempted to charge more money? Those sweating workers might be willing to pay $2 for a cup of cold lemonade. Maybe even $3!

The laws of supply and demand affect all trade, including global trade. Supply is the quantity of goods that people have to sell at a particular price. Demand is the quantity of goods people are willing to buy at a particular price. In a perfect world, supply and demand would be equal. Sellers have the exact quantity of goods that buyers want to buy at a certain price. When supply and demand are not equal, the price of goods can change.

Let's consider another scenario. Assume the price of a table is $200. At that price, those who make the table, the producers, are willing to make 100 tables because they can sell them and make a good profit.

But what if buyers are only willing to purchase 50 tables at the $200 price? To get rid of the remaining 50 tables, the producer lowers the price to $70. At the new price, buyers are willing to purchase the remaining 50 tables. In this example, supply was greater than demand. It caused the price of the table to drop.

Sometimes, demand is greater than supply. The table maker again makes 100 tables to sell at $200. This time, 150 people want to buy the tables. There are more buyers than tables available. Some of the buyers offer $225 to the table maker, who accepts the offer and sells all of the tables at the higher price. In this case, demand was greater than supply and caused the table's price to rise.

TRADE IMBALANCES

A trade balance is the difference between exports and imports. Exports produce income for a country and add to the trade balance. Imports send money to foreign countries to pay for goods and services, reducing the trade balance.

When a country exports more than it imports, it has a trade surplus. When it imports more than it exports, a trade deficit exists. In a perfect world, two countries would buy and sell an equal amount of products from each other. They would have a trade balance. This rarely happens in the real world. Often, one country sells more goods to another country than it buys in return. When this occurs, a trade imbalance exists. Sometimes, a trade imbalance occurs because one country can produce goods more cheaply than another country. Often, this happens because the cost of labor is lower in the country that is selling.

IS TRADE IMBALANCE A PROBLEM?

Some people argue that when a country has a trade deficit, it is sending its money to people in another country and making itself poorer in the process. Also, when a trade deficit exists, a country relies on other countries for necessary goods—high demand for imported products can cause local companies to cut jobs. However, a deficit that lowers the value of a country's currency might encourage foreign investment, and this money can be used to grow businesses, build infrastructure, or pay for other projects in the country. A trade deficit also means that people are buying more goods. When the economy and incomes grow, demand for all goods, including imports, also grows. A growing trade deficit is often a sign of a healthy, growing economy.

Year	Exports	Imports	Balance
2016	1,451,010.7	2,187,804.9	−736,794.2
2015	1,503,101.5	2,248,183.2	−745,081.8
2014	1,621,873.8	2,356,356.1	−734,482.3

U.S. trade in goods with world (in millions of U.S. dollars)

VOCAB LAB

Write down what you think each word means. What root words can you find to help you? What does the context of the word tell you?

barter, **capital**, **comparative advantage**, **currency**, **deficit**, **efficiency**, **profit**, **export**, **import**, **labor**, **supply and demand**, **surplus**, and **trade imbalance**.

Compare your definitions with those of your friends or classmates. Did you all come up with the same meanings? Turn to the text and glossary if you need help.

A trade imbalance might also occur because of the value of each country's currency. At any point in time, a country's currency has a value in the global market. This value determines how much a unit of the currency can buy. When a currency has a high value, it can buy more goods. It is also more desired in the global market.

How does this affect global trade imbalances? If the U.S. dollar is worth more than the Japanese yen in the global market, then Japanese businesses will receive fewer U.S. dollars for their products. This causes the prices of Japanese products to fall for U.S. customers, so they will buy more Japanese goods. In Japan, however, U.S. businesses will need to charge more Japanese yen for their goods. This causes the price of American-made goods in Japan to rise. The Japanese people will buy fewer U.S. goods because of the higher prices.

Globalization has changed the way the global community does business. In communities from Alaska to Shanghai, global trade has opened doors to new goods, people, and ideas. Through trade, people from different cultures and parts of the world can connect more than ever.

KEY QUESTIONS

- What is the theory of competitive advantage and how does it affect global trade?

- What are some of the benefits and drawbacks of being fully reliant on another country for certain products?

- How is a trade imbalance created and should countries try to keep the imbalance small?

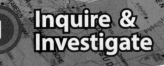
WHY DO PEOPLE TRADE?

Trade is the exchange of goods and services. In this activity, you will investigate and explore the reasons why people and countries trade.

- **Why do people trade?** Write down all of the reasons why people might trade.

- **To test your hypotheses on why people trade, set up a trading experiment.** Recruit your classmates, friends, or family to be trading partners. Each person gets a paper bag with some small items inside, such as candies, gum, pencils, erasers, granola bars, stickers, and more. Some bags will have more of one item, others will have more of another item. Some bags may hold only one type of item. The trading partners can keep whatever they have in their bag at the end of the trading session.

- **Divide your group into two subgroups.** For the first round of trading, each person can trade only with people in their subgroup. Allow participants up to 10 minutes to make their trades.

- **At the end of the trading round, how many participants made at least one trade?** Why did they trade? Do they believe that they are better or worse off after trading? Why? Why did some participants decide not to trade? How did the trade restriction affect trade?

- **Open a second round of trading.** This time, there are no restrictions. How many participants traded this time? How did eliminating the trade restrictions affect trade? Why did participants trade? Do they believe they are better or worse off after trading? Why?

> To investigate more, design a trading scenario where some people have a greater number of items and more valuable items than others. How does this impact trade? Does each person still benefit from trade? How does this example apply to trade between wealthy and poor nations?

WHO IS RESPONSIBLE FOR WORKER SAFETY?

In today's global economy, companies often set up factories in areas with the lowest costs. With some of the lowest wages in the world, Bangladesh has attracted many Western companies, particularly in clothing manufacturing, called the garment industry.

Many American companies, including Walmart and the Gap, have contracted with Bangladesh garment factories to produce clothing.

• **Safety standards in Bangladesh garment factories are not the same as standards in the United States.** This has been highlighted by numerous disasters. You can read about these tragedies at the following websites.

  • "Building Collapse in Bangladesh Leaves Scores Dead"

  🔍 Savar Building Bangladesh 2013

  • "Horrific Fire Revealed a Gap in Safety for Global Brands"

  🔍 Fire safety global brands

• **Some companies have had different responses to the working conditions in Bangladesh.** Learn more about their response.

  • "Some Retailers Rethink Role in Bangladesh"

  🔍 Retailers rethink Bangladesh

• **Should a company withdraw from a country where safety standards are not met or should it stay and try to improve working conditions for the local workers?** Choose a side and research your position. Then, write a persuasive essay explaining your position or debate a classmate who has taken the opposite position.

To investigate more, look at some of the tags on your clothing. Where are your clothes made? Do you as a consumer have any responsibility for workers in other countries who make the clothes you wear? If yes, what can you do?

Chapter 3
The Global Rules of Trade

I WAS THINKING THAT GIVING YOU TWO PEARS ISN'T THAT FAIR.

What do countries do to ensure global trade is fair?

Governments have applied rules and regulations to systems of trade to make sure companies are using the same guidelines when it comes to global trade.

● ● ● ● ● ● ● ● ● ● ● ●

The world of trade has come a long way since early people exchanged beads for textiles. Products and services are traded around the world between big businesses, small businesses, individuals, nonprofit groups, and a number of other entities. How do governments make sure that everything is fair? How do they ensure that no one business or country gains a monopoly?

When countries import goods, the demand for locally made goods might decline. If this happens, local economies make less money, and workers could lose their jobs. A town that is home to a factory where 1,000 people work will suffer if the company goes out of business or moves.

If it can't compete with products made in China, a company might decide to move its operations to another country where labor is cheaper. What would happen to the stores, restaurants, doctors' practices, and other places of business if 1,000 people lost their jobs and no longer had money to spend?

PUTTING UP TRADE BARRIERS

To protect companies and workers, governments often try to manage trade in two basic ways: by restricting imports and encouraging exports. They put policies and regulations in place that make it easier and cheaper for people to buy local products. These regulations are known as trade barriers because they slow or limit the flow of goods between two countries.

One of the most common barriers to trade is a tariff. A tariff is a fee charged on every imported good, usually calculated as a percentage of the import's value. For example, if the United States imposes a 10-percent tariff on imported French wine, then a retailer bringing a $100 shipment of French wine into the United States will have to pay a $10 tariff to the U.S. government.

To recover the tariff's cost, the importing company will usually increase the price of the wine to American buyers. Tariffs can therefore make imported goods more expensive than locally made goods, which makes people more likely to buy domestic products.

TRUE NEWS

The United States and its allies have trade restrictions on the export of weapons, military technology, and other technologies with possible military use to countries suspected of developing weapons of mass destruction.

This chart shows a history of the United States' trade imbalance with China.

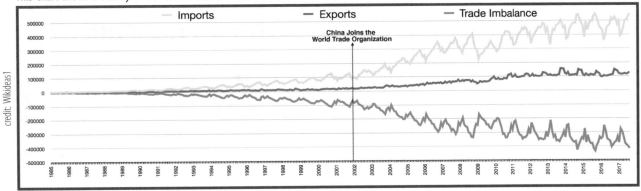

credit: Wikideas1

A government can also influence trade through subsidies. A subsidy is an amount of money the government pays to a local company. This money helps the company produce its goods and charge customers lower prices. When the local company can charge a lower price, it can better compete with foreign imports.

A quota limits the quantity of a particular good that can be imported. By limiting access to imports, quotas make a product scarce. The government is trying to ensure that any demand for a good for more than the quota amount is filled by domestic producers instead of foreign producers. In the 1980s, the United States imposed a quota on sugar imports. The quota was put in place to protect American sugar producers that faced competition from lower-priced, foreign suppliers.

An embargo is a complete ban on the trade of a certain good or with a specific country. In 1962, President John F. Kennedy declared a trade embargo between the United States and Cuba because of the Cuban government's ties to the communist Soviet Union. A version of the trade embargo still exists today, making it one of the longest trade embargos in U.S. history. Have you heard stories about trade embargoes in the news?

OTHER CONSEQUENCES

While tariffs, subsidies, and quotas give an advantage to domestic companies and workers, they can also have some negative effects. Import tariffs and quotas raise the prices of imported goods for consumers. In addition, when local producers do not have to compete with foreign producers, they can charge higher prices to local customers.

Subsidies make it easier for local companies to sell their products at cheaper prices and still make a good profit. They can also export their goods to other countries at these low prices. Producers in these countries can suffer, which means workers could lose their jobs.

What can some of these negative effects look like in real life? In 2011, the Argentinian government imposed a 35-percent tariff on imported cell phones, computers, and tablets. The tariff was designed to protect manufacturing workers in Argentina.

Companies that manufactured products in Argentina would not be subject to the tariff. The government hoped that this would encourage foreign companies to set up manufacturing plants in Argentina, which would bring many benefits, including employing more workers.

> While some companies did expand manufacturing to Argentina, others, including Apple, did not. As a result, Argentina became one of the world's most expensive places to buy Apple products, such as iPhones and iPads.

The high prices caused many stores to stop selling Apple products. Because Argentinian consumers still wanted these products, they turned to the black market or went online to buy them. Some even traveled to nearby Chile to buy Apple products at lower prices.

In 2017, the Argentinian government announced that it would remove the tariff on imported computers and tablets. It is expected to remove tariffs on cell phones in the coming months.

Governments sometimes use sanctions to restrict imports and exports for political reasons. A sanction is a trade restriction that is meant to punish or influence another country for human rights violations or acts of aggression.

DRAWBACKS

Import restrictions and export subsidies can also discourage local companies from becoming more efficient in order to compete better globally. Instead, they rely on government support and subsidies to survive and profit.

REDUCING TRADE BARRIERS

Many people feel that the global market would be better off if trade barriers were removed. Without trade barriers, it would be easier and cheaper for people around the world to get the goods they want and need.

However, removing trade barriers is often very tricky.

What if one country removes its trade barriers but another does not? Countries without the barriers could be hurt when foreign competitors sell goods at cheaper prices. In addition, because their goods would still be subject to tariffs and quotas, they would have a harder time exporting goods. To protect themselves, countries typically enter into trade agreements that require all parties to reduce trade barriers. With these agreements, importing and exporting goods can be easier for all participating countries.

WTO

After World War II, many countries wanted to encourage international trade. They believed that trade among nations would help each nation rebuild its infrastructure and economy after the long, hard war.

Members of the WTO

Members

Members, dually represented by the European Union

Observers

Non-members

In 1947, 23 countries signed the General Agreement on Trade and Tariffs (GATT). The agreement reduced industrial tariffs, quotas, and other trade restrictions. More countries gradually joined GATT. Changes to the original agreement reduced trade barriers even more. By 1994, 123 nations had signed the agreement.

The countries that had signed GATT agreed that a formal organization was needed to deal with global trade issues. The result was the World Trade Organization (WTO). Like GATT, the WTO works to reduce trade barriers. While GATT was a set of rules for global trade, the WTO is an organization that regulates international trade. It works to ensure that trade between countries flows smoothly. The WTO is run by its member governments. As of July 2016, there were 164 member countries.

While the WTO was created to promote free trade, critics claim the organization has favored certain countries over others—in particular, developed countries at the expense of poorer, less-developed nations.

Formed in 1995, the WTO acts as a forum for multilateral trade negotiation, administers multilateral trade agreements, rules on trade disputes, and reviews national trade policies.

• • • • • • • • • • • •

TRUE NEWS

The practice of helping a country's industries by placing tariffs on competitive foreign imports is called protectionism.

Protesting WTO policies in Jakarta, Indonesia

credit: Jonathan McIntosh

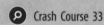
Without some trade protections, developing countries are often unable to start new industries or diversify into other industries. Workers in poor nations are often exploited to produce cheap goods that benefit rich corporations and countries.

In addition, some people claim that the WTO and its free-trade policies do not consider the environment. Free trade allows countries with minimal environmental protections in place to export goods around the world. Others believe the WTO's free-trade policies reduce cultural diversity and encourage the growth of large, multinational corporations.

TRADE TREATIES

Smaller groups of nations have also joined together in regional trading blocs to increase trade. Trade agreements have been made among countries in North America, Europe, Southeast Asia, South America, Central America, and Africa. While each agreement is different, all the agreements have a common goal: to increase trade and prosperity in the participating countries by reducing trade barriers.

In 1993, the creation of the European Union (EU) reduced trade barriers among its member countries. The EU also made trade between countries easier by introducing a single currency called the euro that most member nations use.

The United States participates in several regional trade agreements, including the North American Free Trade Agreement (NAFTA). NAFTA was signed in 1994 and involves the United States, Mexico, and Canada. Under the agreement, the three countries cut import tariffs to zero for almost all manufactured products traded between them.

WHAT'S NICE ABOUT NAFTA?

As with most trade agreements, NAFTA brought advantages and disadvantages. It significantly increased trade among all three countries. Consumers paid lower prices for many goods. Some American industries also experienced gains. For example, American farmers had a new, large market for sales. Even though NAFTA caused some domestically produced goods to be replaced by imported goods, the new markets for each country made up for the loss of domestic production.

> Although NAFTA may be beneficial overall, for some people it has been harmful.

Some American industries, such as the auto industry, shifted manufacturing work to Mexico, where labor was less expensive. This caused the loss of many manufacturing jobs in the United States. And although manufacturing jobs increased in Mexico, they were often low-paying.

In May 2017, the White House notified the U.S. Congress that it intended to renegotiate NAFTA. President Donald Trump (1946–) has indicated that the United States may withdraw entirely from the deal if a satisfactory renegotiation does not occur.

WORLD'S BIGGEST STORE

What do all of these trade regulations and agreements mean for the real world? Have you ever been to a Walmart? In 1962, Walmart opened its first store in Arkansas. By the 1970s, Walmart started to expand across the country and, by the 1990s, Walmart had stores in every area of the United States. It was the country's top retailer.

Walmart Supercenter in Shenzhen, China

BIG MAC INDEX

Every year, the *Economist* magazine publishes the Big Mac Index. This index measures the price of a Big Mac hamburger sold at McDonald's restaurants worldwide. It compares the burger prices to the exchange rate of other currencies. Many experts have found that the Big Mac Index is often a relatively accurate predictor of changes in exchange rates. Check out the Big Mac Index at this website. Which countries offer Big Macs for less money? Which charge more? What do these countries have in common?

🔍 Economist Big Mac

In 1991, Walmart opened its first store in Mexico, then expanded into Canada. In 1996, the company opened its first stores in China.

As it grew into different countries, Walmart used different strategies. In some places, Walmart took over an existing local store or created an alliance with a local business. For example, in Mexico, Walmart formed a 50-50 joint venture with Cifra, Mexico's largest retailer. Cifra provided operational expertise for the Mexican market.

Walmart understood that it needed to adapt to local markets and cultures. In China, Walmart experimented with different store formats and products to see which appealed the most to Chinese customers. Stores were stocked with merchandise mainly manufactured in China by global suppliers or by local producers. This balanced the Chinese government's pressure to sell locally made goods with customers' demands for high-status U.S. goods.

As of 2017, Walmart had more than 11,000 stores operating under multiple banners in 28 countries. It also operated e-commerce websites in 11 countries. Revenue in fiscal year 2017 was $485.9 billion.[1]

CHANGES AND CHALLENGES

As more countries have agreed to reduce trade barriers, global trade flows have multiplied more than 20 times worldwide. Many experts believe this massive explosion in global trade has increased productivity, improved living standards, and increased prosperity around the world.

For already industrialized nations such as the United States, the emergence of new manufacturing countries has been both positive and negative. As the economies of developing nations grow, they have become large markets for U.S. and European exports. These opportunities have benefited many American companies and workers.

> At the same time, the increase in global trade has been difficult for some industries.

Many developing countries have lower labor costs than those in industrialized nations, which gives them an advantage when producing manufactured goods. This has led to an increase in imports of manufactured goods that are cheaper than locally produced goods. As a result, some U.S. companies have gone out of business or moved their manufacturing facilities to developing countries. The loss of jobs for American workers, particularly good-paying manufacturing jobs, has been difficult for many communities.

As with most things, globalization is a mix of positive and negative outcomes. In the next chapter, we'll take a look at how this works in terms of global politics!

VOCAB LAB

Write down what you think each word means. What root words can you find to help you? What does the context of the word tell you?

adapt, **capitalism**, **embargo**, **monopoly**, **protectionism**, **quota**, **subsidy**, **tariff**, and **trade agreement**.

Compare your definitions with those of your friends or classmates. Did you all come up with the same meanings? Turn to the text and glossary if you need help.

KEY QUESTIONS

- **What might the world be like if there were no regulations on international trade?**

- **Do rules and regulations make it easier for organizations to protect the environment?**

WINNERS OR LOSERS?

Global trade has many benefits. It lowers the price of goods, increases wages, and fuels economic growth. Yet the global economy has both winners and losers.

- **To further understand this issue, you can explore the following articles or research some additional information on your own.**

  - "More Wealth, More Jobs, but Not for Everyone: What Fuels the Backlash on Trade"

   Trade backlash

  - "The Toughest Questions About Global Trade"

   CBS global trade 2016

- **Based on what you learn, consider the effects of global trade on individuals, companies, and governments.** For example, think about the effect of global trade on a multinational toy corporation, an American factory worker, a Chinese factory worker, an Indian software engineer, an American chief executive officer, a local toy retailer, the United States government, and the Chinese government. Who are the winners and losers? Create a chart that shows the effects of global trade on the different groups.

- **Do you think that increasing global trade will have a positive, negative, or neutral effect on the world overall?** What about for the United States? Do you believe that the United States should enter into more free-trade agreements? Or do you believe that trade protectionism is a better strategy? Explain your position.

> **To investigate more,** consider that as globalization changes the economy, local workers and businesses can be hurt by disappearing sales and jobs. What policies can the government put in place to support workers and businesses hurt by globalization?

Chapter 4 ▷
Global Politics

How does globalization affect the politics of different countries?

Many governments are working together to make the world a safe, productive, and healthy place for all people to live. Sometimes, governments work together easily, but often there are disagreements that need to be settled in different ways.

• • • • • • • • • • • • •

Countries are responsible for keeping their citizens safe and secure. Each country creates laws and policies that are enforced within its borders. While different political groups may argue and battle for control, activities related to governing have traditionally remained within a country's borders.

As globalization spreads, governments are becoming increasingly connected. Imagine the entire world as a very large city. The city has many parts, all of which are needed to make it work. There are parks, schools, hospitals, apartments, and stores. The people who work in the city include teachers, garbage collectors, doctors, and postal workers.

While each part of the city has its own needs and problems, they are all connected to each other. For example, the stores, schools, and apartment buildings could dispose of their own trash, but it is more efficient if the city's garbage collectors handle this need for the entire city.

In the same way, countries and people around the world are becoming more connected in a global community. Instead of each nation trying to handle its own problems, more countries are realizing the benefits of working together. While individual countries still have an important role in global politics, some countries have created formal agreements to work together. Plus, intergovernmental organizations, nongovernmental organizations (NGOs), and multinational enterprises are taking an increasing role in politics around the world.

WORKING TOGETHER: THE EUROPEAN UNION

In Europe, nations such as France, Italy, and Germany operated independently for centuries. Then, World War II happened, and more than 50 million people died while entire cities were reduced to rubble. The war left tremendous physical and financial destruction across Europe. Could this tragedy happen again? How might people prevent it?

After World War II, several European countries took steps to encourage economic cooperation. European nations wanted to find a way to promote peace and prevent future wars. They believed that increased trade among European countries would make them more economically dependent on each other.

> This, in turn, would make each nation more likely to cooperate with the others to avoid conflict and the devastation of war.

TRUE NEWS

European nations also work together in the Council of Europe, an international organization with 47 member states. Its mission is to uphold human rights, democracy, and rule of law, and promote European culture.

Members countries of the ECSC, 1952

credit: Glentamara

In 1952, six countries—Belgium, Germany, France, Italy, Luxembourg, and the Netherlands—formed the European Coal and Steel Community (ECSC). The main goal of the ECSC was to establish a common market and to increase the trade of coal and steel. The participating countries would pool their coal and steel resources and create a common market by lifting import and export duties. A duty is a tax on imports and exports. The ECSC also aimed to prevent the buildup of resources in any one country that could lead to the rise of a military superpower and to the possibility of war.

The ECSC was the world's first supranational organization, a union in which member countries share in decision making and vote on issues that affect the entire group. For the first time, member nations were governed by laws and policies developed outside their borders and national governments. The ECSC was the beginning of what would eventually become the European Union.

In 1958, the six countries expanded their agreement and established the European Economic Community (EEC). The EEC's goal was to encourage all trade, not just trade of coal and steel. To do this, the member countries created a common market and eliminated barriers to free trade, such as border checks and customs, as if the member nations were part of one country.

Gradually, more countries joined the EEC. Although it originally began as a partnership for trade, the EEC expanded into a variety of different areas. It began to address issues such as protecting the environment and building better roads and railways across Europe. In 1993, the EEC changed its name to the European Union (EU) to reflect its expanded role.

GLOBALIZATION | CHAPTER FOUR

Today, the EU is an economic and political union of 28 countries. Each country remains independent, but has agreed to follow regulations established by the EU. The EU operates a single market in which people, goods, services, and money can move freely, as if the EU were one country. The goal was to boost trade among member nations, create jobs, and lower prices for everyone in the EU.

EU citizens do not need passports to travel within most of the European Union. They can set up businesses or take jobs anywhere within the EU. The EU also maintains diplomatic relations with most countries worldwide. It strives to promote peace and cooperation and strengthen global security around the world.

Member states of the European Union, 2017

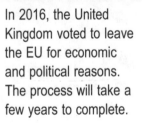

TRUE NEWS

In 2016, the United Kingdom voted to leave the EU for economic and political reasons. The process will take a few years to complete.

While the EU has brought many benefits to members, critics say that it has created too many regulations and has taken away the ability of member countries to control their own affairs. Also, free movement of people has allowed mass migrations of citizens from poorer to richer countries.

MAKING DECISIONS

Everything the EU does is based on treaties agreed to by its member countries. A treaty is a formal and ratified agreement among countries. Through its treaties, EU members have transferred part of their sovereignty, which is their right to govern themselves, to the EU.

> Many political and governing decisions are now made by the EU, instead of by individual nations.

The EU consists of four main institutions: the European Council, the European Parliament, the Council of the European Union, and the European Commission.

- The European Council is made up of 28 heads of government, one for each member country. It meets regularly to set the EU's general strategy and policy agenda.

- The European Parliament is the voice of the people of the EU. Elected by the people every five years, the parliament works with the Council of the European Union to pass laws and adopt the EU's annual budget.

- The Council of the European Union is made up of ministers from each member nation and works with the parliament to pass laws and adopt a budget. It also coordinates economic policies and is involved in international agreements.

- The European Commission proposes legislation and manages the EU's day-to-day business. The Commission also negotiates international trade agreements on behalf of the EU.

THE EURO

When the EEC was founded in 1957, each country had its own currency—France had the French franc, Germany had the German mark, and Italy had the Italian lira, for example. Having different currencies made going across borders more complicated. Imagine taking a tour of Europe and visiting all of these countries—you'd need to get all of these currencies!

Now, imagine doing business with each of these countries—that gets even more complicated. If the value of the currencies changed, companies doing business across borders risked losing money. It also made it more difficult to compare the sale of an item in one country to the sale of the same item in another country.

In 1991, the EU member countries approved the Treaty on European Union, also known as the Maastricht Treaty. With this step, they decided to create a single EU currency, called the euro. In 1999, the EU introduced the euro to world financial markets.

The capital of the EU is located in Brussels, Belgium.

● ● ● ● ● ● ● ● ● ● ● ● ●

THE EURO

Today, the euro is the official currency of 19 of the 28 EU member states. Currently, Bulgaria, Croatia, the Czech Republic, Denmark, Hungary, Poland, Romania, Sweden, and the United Kingdom do not use the euro. Two of these countries, the United Kingdom and Denmark, are legally exempt from ever adopting the euro.

On June 23, 2016, the United Kingdom held a referendum—a vote in which everyone of voting age can participate—to decide if the United Kingdom should leave or stay in the EU. In a close vote, the majority of voters chose to leave the EU. According to EU treaties, any country that wishes to leave the EU can do so by notifying the European Council and negotiating its withdrawal. They have two years to reach a withdrawal agreement, which can be extended if all parties agree. On March 29, 2017, British Prime Minister Theresa May officially notified the European Council of the United Kingdom's desire to leave the EU and triggered the two-year withdrawal process.

The euro has brought both benefits and costs to the EU. Business in the EU is more cost effective with euros since there is one large market that uses the same currency. Businesses can easily compare prices across borders, which encourages trade. Plus, without the risks of changing currency exchange rates, investment is more efficient.

At the same time, a single currency has meant less flexibility for member states. For example, during the financial crisis of 2007–2008, the economies of some EU countries, such as Greece, Spain, Italy, and Portugal, suffered more than other EU countries. Because of the EU's single monetary policy, these nations were not able to set policies that might have sped up their recoveries. For example, they could not adjust interest rates to influence investment or buying decisions.

INTERGOVERNMENTAL ORGANIZATIONS

Intergovernmental organizations (IGO) are another way that different governments work together toward a common goal. An IGO is made up of independent nations, called member states. A treaty or charter establishes the IGO and also defines its purpose and goals. Member states keep their sovereignty.

Some IGOs provide a neutral forum to resolve disputes. Others oversee common interests, such as preserving peace, environmental protection, human rights, and social development. Some organizations offer humanitarian aid and economic development programs to areas in need. The United Nations is one of the most well-known IGOs.

Other IGOs target specific issues. For example, the World Bank Group works to reduce poverty by offering loans to poor countries so that they can improve education, health, or agriculture. The WTO regulates international trade and promotes open markets for all nations. The North Atlantic Treaty Organization (NATO) coordinates defense systems to improve international security.

UNITED NATIONS

The United Nations (UN) is one of the most influential intergovernmental organizations in the world today. From August to October 1944, representatives from China, the Soviet Union, Great Britain, and the United States met to discuss a new international organization to stop future wars and promote cooperation between countries. In 1945, representatives from 50 countries attended the United Nations Conference on International Organization. They established the UN on October 24, 1945.

President Barack Obama addresses the UN General Assembly in New York City in 2009

credit: White House (Samantha Appleton)

TRUE NEWS

In 2012, the EU was awarded the Nobel Peace Prize for advancing the causes of peace, democracy, and human rights in Europe.

HUMAN RIGHTS IN THE EU

One of the EU's main goals is to promote human rights around the world. The EU Charter of Fundamental Rights defines these rights in a single document. All EU institutions and member governments are legally bound to uphold these rights. You can read the Charter of Fundamental Rights at this website.

 EU Charter Rights

The UN Security Council works to maintain international peace and security. It is also responsible for recommending the appointment of the UN leader, called the secretary-general, and for deciding on the admission of new members to the UN.

● ● ● ● ● ● ● ● ● ● ● ●

TRUE NEWS

The secretary-general serves as the UN spokesperson for the interests of the world's peoples, in particular the poor and vulnerable. The current and ninth UN secretary-general is António Guterres (1949–), who was previously the prime minister of Portugal.

The UN is an international organization that works to increase political and economic cooperation among member countries. The Charter of the United Nations (UN Charter) is the United Nations' governing document. It sets out four main goals for the UN.

1. Maintain world peace and security

2. Develop friendly relations among nations

3. Foster cooperation among nations to solve economic, social, cultural, or humanitarian problems

4. Provide a forum for bringing member countries together to meet UN goals

Membership in the UN is open to any country that promotes peace and agrees to be held to the principles in the UN Charter. Almost every country and sovereign state around the world is represented in the UN.

The UN unites the world's nations together for the common goal of peace.

The United Nations performs many important functions. For example, each member nation, regardless of its size or power, has one seat in the General Assembly. The General Assembly conducts studies and makes recommendations on international law, human rights, and international cooperation. It also provides recommendations for peaceful settlement of issues between member nations. In some cases, the General Assembly may be involved in discussing issues related to international peace and security.

A UN soldier waits to distribute pallets of humanitarian aid that are being dropped in Haiti.

credit: Tech. Sgt. James L. Harper Jr., USAF

The UN Economic and Social Council focuses on economic, social, and environmental issues, while the International Court of Justice settles disputes and provides advice.

NONGOVERNMENTAL ORGANIZATIONS

Nongovernmental organizations (NGOs) are not-for-profit groups that are independent from government. They are formed to address issues that affect the public good, such as human rights, humanitarian aid, economic development, social welfare, and the environment. Some well-known NGOs include Amnesty International, Greenpeace, the Red Cross, UNICEF, and Oxfam.

TRUE NEWS

The trick-or-treat for UNICEF program, where kids in the United States collect donations while going door to door on Halloween, has raised more than $175 million since 1950.

NGOs generally fall into two main categories: advocacy NGOs and operational NGOs, although many perform both functions.

● ● ● ● ● ● ● ● ● ● ● ●

Read about Dr. Edward Chu's six months spent with Doctors Without Borders in Bangui, the capital of Central African Republic. How did his experiences overseas affect his work in the United States?

Edward Chu
Bangui

Advocacy NGOs provide a voice for those who do not have one. They advocate on important social issues, such as poverty, human rights, and the environment. Advocacy NGOs often work through campaigning, raising awareness about an issue, developing local support for a cause, fundraising, and lobbying lawmakers.

They also act as watchdogs to monitor for actions that violate human rights. Amnesty International is an advocacy NGO that promotes human rights and watches for human rights abuses throughout the world. It works to hold guilty parties, from governments to private companies, accountable for abusing human rights.

Greenpeace is another advocacy NGO. It advocates for environmental conservation and sustainable practices. Its goals include protecting the world's natural resources and habitats, stopping global warming, and halting the spread of nuclear energy and pollution.

Operational NGOs step in to meet people's needs and provide essential goods and services. Some countries are unable to meet their citizens' basic needs. Sometimes, this happens because the country is too poor or underdeveloped.

Other times, a natural disaster or corrupt leadership wipes out the country's resources.

Some operational NGOs provide financial aid and loans to help improve the economy. Other NGOs help with basic needs, such as medical care, safe water, food, and sanitation.

Doctors Without Borders, also known as Médecins Sans Frontières, is an organizational NGO that provides medical care and training to people in less-developed and war-ravaged countries. In 2013 and 2014, Doctors Without Borders sent thousands of medical staff to West Africa to manage the Ebola virus outbreak.

Another NGO, Oxfam, works to end global poverty. Oxfam provides food, water, and sanitation services during natural disasters, and also works to ensure a global food supply for the poor. In 2017, monsoon rains and heavy flooding in South Asia killed 1,200 people and destroyed thousands of homes and crops. Oxfam stepped in to provide clean drinking water, food supplies, emergency shelter, hygiene kits, and other essentials to more than 186,000 people affected by the flooding.

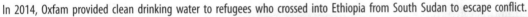

In 2014, Oxfam provided clean drinking water to refugees who crossed into Ethiopia from South Sudan to escape conflict.

credit: Oxfam East Africa

MULTINATIONAL ENTERPRISES

Multinational enterprises or corporations can also influence international politics. These companies have business interests in more than one country. Often, they have vast resources that may even exceed the resources of small countries. Well-known multinational enterprises include IBM, Volvo, General Electric, Exxon Mobil, Samsung, and Boeing.

These corporations can influence governments. They might hire lobbyists to try to persuade lawmakers to take positions on trade policies, taxes, and immigration that are favorable to their businesses. The interests of a multinational corporation do not always match those of the countries where they operate. For example, the corporation may oppose trade sanctions that negatively impact its business.

As countries become more connected, many governments are working together to make the world a better place for all to live. For many people, this increased cooperation has been positive, making communities safer, while also improving health and economies. At the same time, governments working together can create new challenges and disagreements that must be solved in different ways.

VOCAB LAB

Write down what you think each word means. What root words can you find to help you? What does the context of the word tell you?

advocacy, **human rights**, **humanitarian aid**, **intergovernmental**, **lobbyist**, **monetary**, **NGO**, **sovereignty**, **supranational**, **sustainable**, and **treaty**.

Compare your definitions with those of your friends or classmates. Did you all come up with the same meanings? Turn to the text and glossary if you need help.

KEY QUESTIONS

- Do governments always have the best interests of their citizens in mind when they do business with other governments? Why or why not?

- How might the world work with one central government regulating every country? Would this be better or worse? How?

A MEETING OF THE EUROPEAN COUNCIL

The European Council meets regularly to discuss current issues and negotiate the EU's position on these issues. In these meetings, each country must represent its own interests while also coming to an agreement on what is best for the EU as a whole. In this activity, you will simulate a European Council meeting.

- **Review newspapers, magazines, and websites to find a topic that impacts the EU.** Consider the economy, trade, national security, human rights, or the environment.

- **Each participant represents a specific country in the EU.** Research your country's position on the topic you selected and investigate the history, politics, economics, or current demographics of your country.

- **Write a short diplomatic statement that explains your country's position on the topic.**

- **Simulate a European Council meeting to discuss the chosen topic.** Research the procedures that the council uses to run its meetings, including who runs the meeting, how participants are seated, and how to recognize speakers and control debate. Use these guidelines to discuss and debate the topics.

- **How are the positions of the countries on the topic alike and different?** What strategies did you observe during the simulation that helped the group reach a consensus? What are the advantages of working together as a group on the issue? What are the disadvantages?

> **To investigate more,** think about the advantages and disadvantages of being part of the EU. Create a chart that compares both sides. Why would a country want to remain in the EU? What would motivate a country to leave it?

A COMMON CURRENCY

Before the euro was adopted by the EU, each country in Europe had its own currency. When people and companies wanted to buy or sell goods and services in different countries, they had to deal with the complexity of currencies.

- **Imagine that you are going shopping before the euro was adopted.** You have 103 Deutsch marks to spend on the following items:

  - Chocolate from Germany for 10 Deutsch marks

  - Pasta from Italy for 4000 lira

  - A baguette from France for 20 francs

  - Tomatoes from Spain for 200 pesetas

- **To make a purchase from another country, convert the marks into euros and then into the foreign currency.** You will also need to add a 5-percent conversion fee to each transaction. Create a chart that shows each conversion, conversion fee, and the final cost of each item purchased. Use the exchange rates with the euro found at this website.

  🔍 Euro conversion 1998

- **Go shopping again, but this time you have 50 euros to spend.**

  - German chocolate for 5.10 euro

  - Italian pasta for 2.05 euro

  - A French baguette for 3.05 euro

  - Spanish tomatoes for 1.20 euro

- **What benefits did you find in having a single currency?** Do you think it would be helpful to have a single worldwide currency?

To investigate more, think about the relationship between a national currency and national identity. How did moving to the euro affect the national identities of the participating member countries? Did it affect some countries more than others? Why or why not?

Chapter 5 ▷
In the Name of the Law

MAYBE WE NEED TO WRITE DOWN OUR COOKIE/FRUIT AGREEMENT?

What laws have countries decided are critical for the well-being of the human race?

International law covers issues such as global economics, human rights, the environment, and armed conflict. A system of treaties and agreements ties countries together in a mutually beneficial web of consequences.

• • • • • • • • • • • •

Who makes and enforces the laws where you live? If you live in the United States, the U.S. government makes the laws. If you live in Canada, the Canadian government creates laws. Traditionally, countries have the authority to decide what laws they need. Their police forces and judicial systems enforce these laws. This has worked for many years.

In most countries, a government makes the rules that citizens follow. In the United States, national laws are created by the legislature. This is our Congress, which has two chambers, the Senate and the House of Representatives. Laws are interpreted by the judiciary, the system of courts that includes the Supreme Court. Enforcement of U.S. law is by the executive branch of government.

If necessary, the government uses the police to force citizens to obey the law. For example, if someone is driving on the wrong side of the road or breaking the speed limit, the police can stop and fine them.

WHAT IS INTERNATIONAL LAW?

As globalization increases the number of interactions between people and countries, countries are required to rethink what laws are needed. Who should make these laws and how should they be enforced?

> International law begins where a country's national laws end.

International laws govern the way countries behave with each other and, in some cases, how they treat their citizens. Years ago, international law primarily dealt with relations among nations during war and with diplomacy. As the world has become more connected, international law is quickly expanding in scope.

Today's international law covers areas such as trade, bankruptcy, intellectual property, and banking procedures. In addition, governments are cooperating to develop a worldwide criminal code to bring some of the world's most notorious international criminals to justice.

For many years, international law was difficult to enforce. There was no global police force or judicial system to enforce the laws. Today, new global legal institutions, such as the International Criminal Court and the International Court of Justice, have the authority to hear cases involving international law. In some instances, local governments are passing laws that follow international standards, which local police forces can enforce.

TRUE NEWS

As international law expands, some large law firms are entering into partnerships with firms in other countries to create mega practices that can serve global clients on global issues.

HOW IS INTERNATIONAL LAW CREATED?

Who makes international rules? The world does not have a single, unified government or legislature to create and enforce international laws. Instead, countries agree to act or not act in certain ways. There are two main sources of international laws: treaties and customary practice.

Treaties are the strongest and most official statements of international law. A treaty is a formal agreement between two or more countries. Treaties are like contracts in which the promises that countries make to each other are formalized in writing and signed by representatives of each country. Countries make treaties that cover any number of areas—from trade to the control of nuclear weapons.

The Peace Palace at The Hague in the Netherlands, where the International Court of Justice is seated

Treaties can be signed by two countries in an agreement that is called bilateral, or by many countries, which is called multilateral. The written provisions of a treaty are binding, which means the signing countries can be held to the promises made in the agreement. Some treaties have their own rules for how they are enforced, while others are enforced by another agency, such as the International Court of Justice. The advantage of treaties is that they can be created quickly and clearly explain the law being created. A drawback, however, is that a treaty only binds those countries that agree to sign it.

Another way to create international law is through customary practice. Customary practices are established behaviors that a community has developed and accepts as rules. Countries have certain customs that have been developed and followed for many years.

Unlike a treaty, a customary law is not a formal agreement. Instead, it is based on what countries and leaders agree to do. When followed for long enough, these customs sometimes become international law.

For example, the law of diplomatic immunity protects diplomats such as ambassadors from being arrested or prosecuted in the countries where they are posted. This practice started as a custom, but is now part of international law. If a country harms a visiting diplomat, other countries see it as a violation of international law. All countries are bound to follow the law, even if they do not specifically consent to it. However, one of the weaknesses of customary international law is that it can be unclear and cause disputes.

WHAT IS THE FOCUS OF INTERNATIONAL LAW?

Much of international law focuses on four main areas: armed conflict, economics and trade, the environment, and human rights. These are areas that we, as a global society, have decided are the most vital to our existence.

Many laws govern actions before, during, and after a war. Some laws cover the legitimate reasons for starting a war, while other laws outline acceptable behavior during war. For example, international law recognizes that a country has the right to use force against another nation when acting in self-defense. In addition, international law states that self-defense actions should be proportional to the attack to which a country is responding. Yet interpreting these laws can be complex. What events justify self-defense? Who decides what is proportional?

NUCLEAR NON-PROLIFERATION TREATY

The Nuclear Non-Proliferation Treaty (NPT) is a landmark multilateral treaty aimed at preventing the spread of nuclear weapons and weapons technology. It also aims to promote cooperation on the peaceful use of nuclear energy and to achieve nuclear disarmament around the world. The NPT went into effect in 1970 and was extended indefinitely in 1995. In total, 191 nations have signed the treaty, including the five nuclear weapons states of China, France, Russia, the United Kingdom, and the United States. Why do you think this is an issue that sparks cooperation across the globe?

Four UN members have not accepted the NPT, including three that have nuclear weapons—India, Israel, and Pakistan. North Korea, which openly declared it has nuclear weapons, withdrew from the NPT in 2003.

Some people believe a country should attack in self-defense only if it has been physically attacked by another country. Others believe self-defense includes pre-emptive strikes against aggressive targets to prevent them from developing into a military threat. Once armed conflict begins, international humanitarian laws apply. Many of these laws are part of the Geneva Conventions, a series of treaties on the treatment of civilians, prisoners of war, and the wounded and sick during wartime.

Some international laws focus on economic matters—they set rules for how nations and multinational companies deal with each other. These laws create rules and regulations for trade, monetary policy, investments, and more. They set a level playing field so that everyone operates under the same rules.

> Some laws regulate transactions by private companies, while others apply to trade agreements between nations.

Other international laws deal with the environment. What do you know about climate change and global warming? These are issues that affect everyone on Earth. Many people around the world understand that the globe has limited resources that should be protected by all nations, regardless of where a resource is physically located. International environmental laws bring countries to work together on issues such as sustainable development, biodiversity, endangered species, hazardous materials, climate change, and pollution. Treaties such as the UN Convention on Biological Diversity and the Convention on International Trade in Endangered Species are examples of this type of international law.

TRUE NEWS

For a state to be bound by a treaty, the state must ratify it, or officially consent to be bound by that treaty. Simply signing a treaty is not ratifying it.

Watch a UN video about the world's biodiversity at this website. Why is this a global issue? How can countries do more by working together instead of working independently?

 UN biodiversity

INTERNATIONAL HUMAN RIGHTS LAWS

While some international law governs the relationships among countries, human rights law governs how a country treats its own citizens.

The UN Charter and the Universal Declaration of Human Rights are the core of international human rights law. After World War II, the world was stunned by the genocide committed by Nazi Germany. For the first time in history, the international community agreed that serious violations of human rights should not be tolerated. It acknowledged that protecting human rights was not the responsibility of a single country, but was the responsibility of the entire world. The UN decided that a strong and unified declaration against human rights violations was needed to prevent future violations from happening.

On December 10, 1948, the UN adopted the Universal Declaration of Human Rights (UDHR). The UDHR lists, for the first time, the fundamental human rights that are to be universally protected. After the UDHR was issued, the UN called upon all member countries to publicize it so that the information could be shared, displayed, read, and discussed in schools and other educational institutions around the world. Although the UDHR is not a legally binding document, it has become a standard for countries around the world to follow.

As time passed, the UN has expanded human rights law to include specific standards and laws that protect women, children, people with disabilities, minorities, and other vulnerable groups from discrimination.

THE GENEVA CONVENTIONS

The Geneva Conventions are a series of treaties that deal with the treatment of civilians, prisoners of war, and sick and wounded soldiers during wartime. The first Geneva Convention was adopted in 1864. It stated that participating countries would care for all sick and wounded military personnel, regardless of nationality. In addition, medical personnel would be considered neutral and identified by a red cross on a white background. This agreement became the foundation of international humanitarian law. Shortly after World War II, the Geneva Conventions were expanded to include military personnel shipwrecked at sea, along with prisoners of war and civilians under enemy control. Rules have also been added to protect cultural objects and places of worship and to ban the recruitment of child soldiers.

International treaties and agreements protect human rights for people around the world. Many agencies have formed to enforce human rights laws, including Amnesty International and Human Rights Watch.

Typically, countries are expected to prosecute offenders who commit human rights violations within their borders. International agencies, such as the UN or the International Criminal Court, only get involved when the country cannot or will not prosecute. For example, the UN is investigating human rights violations carried out on the people of Syria during its civil war. The Syrian government and the rebels fighting the government have been known to conduct mass killings and use chemical weapons on civilians.

Established in 2006, the UN Human Rights Council is made up of 47 countries and works to promote and protect human rights around the world. The council addresses human rights violations and makes recommendations to the UN, including responses to human rights emergencies.

Listen to Eleanor Roosevelt, human rights activist and the First Lady from 1933 to 1945, read from the UDHR. Roosevelt was instrumental in drafting the declaration. Why is this document important? Do you think it's any more or less important now than it was when it was written after World War II?

Roosevelt human rights audio

You can also read the UDHR here.

Universal Declaration Human Rights

credit: National Archives

Every four years, the Human Rights Council reviews the human rights records of all 192 UN member states. The goal of this review is to improve human rights in every country. To achieve this, the review assesses each country's human rights records and addresses human rights violations wherever they occur.

ENFORCEMENT WITH TRIBUNALS

Countries have police and courts to enforce their laws. But who enforces international laws? How do we ensure that countries around the world follow international law?

After World War II, the Allied powers—the United States, Great Britain, Soviet Union, and France—authorized an international military tribunal to prosecute Nazi officials for war crimes and other crimes against humanity. The tribunal was given jurisdiction over offenses that had no particular geographic location, crimes against human dignity, and crimes against specific persons.

The Allies conducted trials at Nuremberg, one of the few German cities that was not in ruins from the war. The trials of leading German officials opened on November 20, 1945, before the international military tribunal.

> Twenty-four Nazi leaders were indicted on charges of crimes against peace, war crimes, crimes against humanity, and conspiracy.

Twenty-two of these men stood trial in Nuremberg. On October 1, 1946, the judges returned their verdict. Twelve men were sentenced to death by hanging. Seven defendants were sentenced to prison, while three were acquitted.

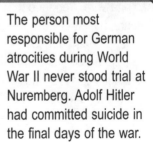

TRUE NEWS

The person most responsible for German atrocities during World War II never stood trial at Nuremberg. Adolf Hitler had committed suicide in the final days of the war.

Defendants at the Nuremberg Trials

credit: U.S. Army

UN SECURITY COUNCIL

The UN Security Council is responsible for maintaining international peace and security. It is the only UN body that can authorize the use of force to implement the council's decisions.

The Security Council is made up of five permanent members: China, France, Russia, the United Kingdom, and the United States. In addition, 10 non-permanent members are elected to two-year terms. In order for a proposal to pass, it must be approved by at least nine members. Every member of the Security Council has one vote. Permanent members, however, have the ability to veto any proposal. If a permanent member votes against a proposal, it will not be adopted.

Similar trials were held in Tokyo to prosecute suspected Japanese war criminals. The Nuremberg and Tokyo tribunals provided a model for how war crimes, crimes against humanity, and other crimes could be prosecuted under international law. Since then, the UN has used tribunals to prosecute war crimes and genocide.

INTERNATIONAL CRIMINAL COURT

While tribunals can be used to enforce international law, they are generally temporary and set up to prosecute only a specific set of crimes. Some nations called for a permanent court to try cases involving war crimes, crimes against humanity, and genocide.

The International Criminal Court (ICC) was the result of a 2002 treaty called the Rome Statute. The ICC became the first permanent court for bringing to justice people who commit serious war crimes.

The ICC prosecutes individuals rather than nations. Unlike tribunals, the ICC is independent from the UN. The ICC takes cases from any country, but can act only in cases where nations are unwilling or unable to prosecute themselves. It also tries only cases involving the most serious crimes, including genocide, war crimes, and crimes against humanity.

As of 2017, 123 countries have ratified the Rome Statute. Some nations—including China, India, and the United States—have not ratified the Rome Statute or supported the ICC. These nations are concerned that the ICC may use its jurisdiction to conduct politically motivated prosecutions of their military and political personnel.

INTERNATIONAL COURT OF JUSTICE

The International Court of Justice (ICJ) is the judicial body responsible for resolving disputes between nations on questions of international law. The ICJ works to resolve conflicts peacefully that in the past might have led to hostilities. The court is made up of judges from 15 different nations and meets in The Hague, in the Netherlands. The ICJ conducts hearings and trials and issues legal opinions.

In one example, the ICJ heard a case that involved a territorial dispute between Israel and Palestine. Israel had built a wall in the West Bank territory to protect itself from suicide bombers.

ICC VERDICT

In 2012, the ICC handed down its first verdict against Thomas Lubanga, the leader of a militia in the Democratic Republic of Congo. The Court convicted Lubanga of war crimes related to the use of children in the country's conflict. He was sentenced to 14 years in prison.

Former child soldiers in the Democratic Republic of Congo

credit: L. Rose of the U.S. Agency for International Development

Palestine argued that the wall violated international law. The ICJ agreed and issued an opinion that the wall hindered Palestine's right to self-determination, meaning its ability to freely decide its political status and freely pursue its economic, social, and cultural development. The ICJ's decisions, however, are non-binding, and Israel challenged the ICJ's authority in the case.

OTHER ENFORCEMENT METHODS

Some treaties have their own enforcement provisions defined in the document itself. Sometimes, a treaty resolves disputes through arbitration, a process where all parties present evidence supporting their claims to neutral mediators who make a binding decision. Other times, a dispute is referred to the ICJ to be resolved. When no enforcement method is defined, countries must use other methods to punish nations for not following international law, including reciprocity, collective action, and shaming.

If a country commits an offense against another country, it can expect the other country to retaliate with the same behavior. Simply knowing this can make countries think carefully about their actions. For example, one country will not kill prisoners from an enemy country if it does not want its own prisoners killed in retaliation. In trade, one country will not put high tariffs in place on another nation's goods if it believes the other nation will retaliate with similar tariffs on its goods.

International law can also be enforced through collective action. Collective action occurs when several nations act together against an offending country to punish it.

TRUE NEWS

The ICJ, which is sometimes called the World Court, rules on disputes between governments but cannot prosecute individuals.

Reciprocity is based on the idea that "what goes around, comes around." Have you heard this expression? What does it mean to you?

• • • • • • • • • • •

Iraqi forces burned oil fields in Kuwait, causing major environmental and economic damage.

credit: Jonas Jordan, U.S. Army Corps of Engineers

When Iraq invaded the neighboring country of Kuwait in 1990, many countries around the world were upset. Working together through the UN, they condemned the invasion and coordinated joint military action to remove Iraqi forces from Kuwait.

Countries have also collectively imposed economic sanctions against a country. Economic sanctions are commercial and financial penalties, including trade barriers, tariffs, and restrictions on financial transactions. To push South Africa to eliminate apartheid, the practice of systematic racial segregation, the UN imposed economic sanctions on South Africa in the 1980s.

SOVEREIGNTY

For centuries, nations have been sovereign, possessing the right to create their own rules and handle their own affairs. As interactions between nations have increased and grown more complex, the nations of the world must learn how to best work together.

THE INFLUENCE OF SHAMING

An effective enforcement tactic is shaming. Most countries do not like to be the target of negative publicity. Therefore, the threat of shaming can influence a nation's actions. Shaming is particularly effective when it involves matters of human rights. Nations that do not want to directly intervene in another country's domestic matters may publicly call attention to violations of international law.

Write down what you think each word means. What root words can you find to help you? What does the context of the word tell you?

arbitration, bilateral, biodiversity, diplomat, genocide, judicial, jurisdiction, justice, multilateral, prosecute, ratify, reciprocate, tribunal, and **veto**.

Compare your definitions with those of your friends or classmates. Did you all come up with the same meanings? Turn to the text and glossary if you need help.

All nations must discover the best way to balance their sovereignty with the good of the international community.

Sovereignty is the full right and power of a nation over itself—the people and property within its borders. Regardless of size, population, or economic status, all nations have the same rights to decide what happens inside their borders. And one nation does not have the right to interfere with the way another nation runs itself. This means that one nation cannot force another nation to take a specific action inside its own country.

Globalization is changing this idea of state sovereignty. Many countries view human rights as a global concern, not an individual country's issue. Through international treaties, more countries are giving up parts of their sovereignty to give their citizens basic rights that are agreed upon by the global community. Countries are working together for a more just and healthy global community.

KEY QUESTIONS

- Why is the environment one of the issues that the majority of the countries of the world are concerned about?

- What might the world be like if human rights were not respected? Has this ever been the case in human history?

- What do you think is the future of human rights? Do you think that people will decide other issues are more important?

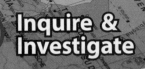

INTERNATIONAL LAW IN THE NEWS

Stories that involve international law are in the news every day. In this activity, you will identify international law news stories and investigate the laws that apply to the issue.

- **Read through a current newspaper.** Identify several stories that involve international law. These can include the following:

  - Bombings
  - Terrorism
  - Children or youth
  - International business
  - Environmental protections
  - Human rights

  - War or conflict
  - International crime or criminals
  - Refugees
  - International trials or tribunals
  - Sanctions
  - Protests

- **Choose one or two stories to investigate.** Consider the following questions.

  - What international law applies to the issues in the article?

  - Do you think this issue should be governed by international law or handled domestically? Explain why.

  - How is this law being enforced?

  - Why was this method of enforcement chosen and do you think it is effective? Explain.

> **To investigate more,** think about arguments against international law, especially as it applies to this issue in particular. Why would a country object to the law and its enforcement? How does the law affect a country's sovereignty?

HUMAN RIGHTS TREATIES

The UDHR has inspired additional treaties and agreements that protect human rights. On the UN website, there are nine core international human rights instruments. Each one is monitored by a committee of experts to ensure the treaty's provisions are being implemented and followed by the states that have signed.

- **You can see a list of these nine core human rights instruments on the UN website.** OHCHR

- **Choose one of the instruments to explore in more detail.** Use the internet and other sources to learn more about the instrument. Consider the following questions.

  - What is the name of your treaty?

  - When did the treaty come into force?

  - What rights does the treaty protect?

  - List three specific rights or freedoms guaranteed by the treaty.

  - Is there a committee that oversees and monitors the treaty? What are the committee's responsibilities?

  - How has this treaty been used in international law?

  - Have any international organizations used the treaty to advocate for the rights of certain people?

- **Prepare a presentation to share what you have learned about the treaty for your class.**

> **To investigate more,** how has the treaty you learned about been enforced? What organizations are involved in enforcement? Has enforcement been successful? Why or why not?

Chapter 6 ▶
Crossing the Cultural Divide

THANKS FOR MEETING, EVERYONE. LET THE FAIR TRADE TALKS BEGIN!

How is culture affected by globalization?

As the world becomes more integrated, different traditions and ways of life are influenced by the outside world. For some communities, this can be a beneficial thing as opportunities develop, but there's also the danger of losing specific cultures to an encroaching wave of Westernization.

· · · · · · · · · · · · ·

Have you ever traveled to another country? Where did you go? Whether you went to Mexico, Belgium, or China, you might have noticed some things that you would find in your hometown, such as a McDonald's fast food restaurant or Coca Cola in stores. You might hear music by Beyoncé on the radio or see people wearing Levi's jeans. These are just a few examples of how culture is spreading and mixing throughout the world.

Culture is a set of values, practices, beliefs, interests, and customs shared by a group of people. That group can be a few hundred people living in a small town or millions of citizens of a country. In addition to spreading goods and services around the world, globalization exposes people to new ideas and experiences. In many cases, people adopt some of these new ideas, which can cause their own cultural values and traditions to change.

Globalization has opened the door to more interactions between cultures than at any other time in history. Some people believe that creating a global culture is good, bringing the people of the world together and helping all of us understand one another better. Other people are not so sure. They believe that globalization is causing the permanent loss of valuable local cultures and traditions.

CULTURAL GLOBALIZATION

Cultural globalization is the process by which one culture's traditions, values, and ideas spread throughout the world. Often, it occurs through the sharing of language, arts, food, business ideas, technology, and pop culture.

For example, people in the United States enjoy listening to South African music and reading Japanese comic books. Have you ever looked at a manga book? India's film industry, known as "Bollywood," creates movies that are popular in India and other countries, including the United States and the United Kingdom. American television shows are popular in Europe and other countries.

Clothing and fashion have also become globalized. Today, fewer people dress in national and regional traditional clothing. When was the last time you saw a Scottish man wearing a kilt? In many parts of the world, business professionals usually wear suits, while young people often dress in jeans and T-shirts, no matter where they live.

SPICY PEPPERS

Today, foods in many parts of China and Korea are very spicy—they get their heat from fiery chili peppers. Yet food was not always this spicy in Asia. In fact, the chili pepper did not exist in Asia before the 1600s because the plant is native to the Western Hemisphere. In the late 1400s, explorer Christopher Columbus first brought chilies to Europe from his journeys to the Americas. As people traveled from Europe to Asia, the spicy peppers arrived in Asia. Gradually, the Asian people incorporated chilies into their recipes, giving their food its well-known spice and heat.

Food is another example of cultural globalization. People in England eat Indian foods, while people in Argentina enjoy Japanese sushi. At the same time, American fast food chains have spread throughout the world. In particular, the worldwide expansion of McDonald's has become a symbol of globalization.

After starting out as an American restaurant in the 1950s, McDonald's first spread across the United States, and later across the world. Today, more than 36,000 McDonald's restaurants thrive in more than 100 countries. Menu items such as the Big Mac are the same all over the world. Globalization has brought McDonald's to billions of people. What do you think this means for people's diets?

A TWO-WAY STREET

The United States' long history of immigration has brought a constant stream of new ideas, cultures, and traditions into the country. It began with the first colonial settlers, from France, Spain, the Netherlands, and Great Britain. It later expanded to include immigrants from China, Eastern Europe, Italy, Germany, Africa, and South America.

Did your family immigrate from a different country? Which one?

People have embraced ideas from other cultures, especially related to food. Italian, Chinese, French, Thai, and Mexican food are widely popular in many regions of the country. Moroccan, Korean, Vietnamese, Cuban, and Peruvian foods are all growing in popularity. In fact, according to one survey, 77 percent of Americans eat ethnic foods at least once a month, and more than one-third eat ethnic food weekly.[1]

The Statue of Liberty has long been seen as an icon of welcome for foreign immigrants to the United States.

credit: National Park Service

Americans have also adopted customs and language from other cultures. Have you ever sung karaoke? This is a form of entertainment developed by the Japanese. Have you swung at a piñata at a birthday party? Piñata have been part of Mexican culture for centuries, after being brought to Mexico by the Spanish. Do you put your thumb up to signal "Okay?" That's a Western custom now used by people around the world.

CAUSES OF CULTURAL GLOBALIZATION

What causes cultural globalization? How do the ideas and traditions of one culture spread to another? Traditionally, ideas and culture have expanded when people—explorers, tourists, or businesspeople—travel from one country to another. These visitors share their own ideas and customs with local people. They also bring back foreign ideas and culture to their home country.

Advances in transportation, technology, and communication have speeded up the exchange of ideas between cultures. It is easier than ever for people to travel to different countries and share culture with the people they meet. Even without physical travel, the internet, cell phones, and social media instantly connect people around the world. People can go online to learn about people and cultures across the globe. If you are going on vacation to another country, what's the first thing you might do? Search the internet!

Traditional media outlets, such as television and newspapers, also spread cultural globalization. Today, news organizations often establish regional branches that expand a particular worldview to new regions.

TRUE NEWS

Foreign words such as "taco," "kindergarten," "croissant," and "café" are regularly used by people across the United States.

For example, the United States' CNN and Great Britain's BBC news organizations have international branches that spread Western perspectives around the world. After starting as a cable news network in the United States, CNN now reaches more than 200 million households in more than 200 countries and territories. At the same time, RT, a Russian news organization, and Al Jazeera, a Middle Eastern news organization, have Western divisions that offer their countries' views on world events.

> The entertainment industry also plays a significant role in the spread of culture.

Hollywood movies and television shows are seen by millions of people around the world. These films and their portrayal of American life, values, and culture have a significant influence on culture around the world. Western celebrities reach a global audience of millions with pictures of their latest outfits or their opinions on current events and important causes.

RIPPLE EFFECTS

Cultural globalization has brought many benefits to people worldwide. For example, people have a deeper understanding and empathy for members of other cultures. Every day, people use the internet to learn about tribal cultures in Africa or to chat online with people from Indonesia. Schoolchildren in Africa can skype with an author living in England.

Yet while globalization increases our understanding of other cultures, it can also promote stereotypes. For example, many people around the world think that all Americans are rich. People who live in the United States know that is certainly not true.

ON SCREEN

One way in which the world is affected by Western culture is through television and movie screens. The entertainment industry distributes American television shows and movies to homes and theaters worldwide. In 2016, many of the most-viewed televisions shows, including *The Walking Dead*, *Pretty Little Liars*, and *The Big Bang Theory*, were American shows. In 2016, the top-grossing movie was *Captain America: Civil War*, which earned more than $1.1 billion worldwide. In fact, all of the movies in the top 10 worldwide box office were Hollywood-made films, including *Rogue One: A Star Wars Story* and *Finding Dory*.

A Burger King restaurant in South Korea

credit: Siqbal

Where did so many people get this idea? American movies and television shows promote the stereotype of the rich American. Televisions shows from the 1990s and today, such as *The Fresh Prince of Bel Air*, *Dallas*, and *Gossip Girl*, showcase the comfortable lives of wealthy Americans. What other popular television shows portray a lifestyle that belongs to only a very few people?

Critics of globalization also argue it threatens the diversity of individual cultures. Each culture has traditions, beliefs, and customs that make it unique and different from other cultures around the world.

As the world is linked together by technology and transportation, some of these differences are fading as people adopt practices and ideas they have learned from other cultures. The world's largest and most dominant cultures are becoming larger and more influential, often at the expense of smaller, local cultures. In particular, critics are concerned that Western cultures, specifically American culture, are taking over the world.

Watch this video to hear why Chinese youth find Western culture attractive. How can sports and fashion continue to be part of the improvement of relations between countries?

 China Youth PBS 2012

WESTERNIZATION OF CULTURE

GLOBAL HOLLYWOOD

Although many people think of Hollywood movies as an American industry, they actually integrate elements from different cultures. Many American movies are remakes of foreign films. Walt Disney's *The Parent Trap* was a remake of a German film called *Two Times Lotte*, which was based on a German book, *Lottie and Lisa*, by Erich Kastner. The movie *The New Adventures of Pippi Longstocking* was based on a series of children's books by Swedish author Astrid Lindgren. In addition, many film companies, producers, directors, actors, and film crew are not American. Columbia Tristar is owned by Sony, a Japanese company. James Cameron, director of *Titanic*, *Avatar*, and *The Terminator*, is Canadian. Many actors are also foreign-born, including *Thor*'s Chris Hemsworth, and *Wonder Woman*'s Gal Gadot.

What would the world be like if every place felt like America? For some people, this is a major concern, as Western traditions and customs are being adopted worldwide. Large American companies have opened stores and restaurants in countries around the world. American films, television shows, books, and music can be found everywhere, from a village in Peru to a high-rise in Hong Kong.

The overwhelming presence of Western and American culture around the world has led to concerns about Westernization or Americanization having a negative effect on local cultures. People around the world own Apple iPhones, wear Levi's jeans, drink Coke, and eat McDonald's Big Macs. English is often the common language used in international business and professional contacts.

Critics point out that globalization is forcing people around the world to become more similar. Diverse cultures could lose their own ideas, languages, and customs as they are replaced by popular Western culture.

Concerns that local cultures are becoming Americanized have led some governments to intervene. In France, local radio stations are required by law to play French songs at least 35 percent of the time. In addition, France requires television programming to be at least 40-percent French and 60-percent European.

By limiting the amount of American content that plays on radios and televisions, the government hopes to preserve local French culture. However, some people oppose these quotas because they limit the choices people have.

TERRORISM AND GLOBALIZATION

In recent years, there has been a backlash against cultural globalization. Some people, especially those who live in the Middle East and Africa, feel as if Western and American culture and values are being forced on them. In fact, many terrorist groups believe that Western influence is harmful to Muslim society. Groups such as Al-Qaeda resent Western culture and believe the United States and the United Kingdom are trying to dominate the world, with both military and economic forces.

For the September 11, 2001, attack on the Twin Towers in New York City, terrorists flew airplanes into strategic U.S. targets.

credit: Mike Goad

It is estimated that approximately 370 million indigenous peoples live around the world. As commonly defined, indigenous people are the descendants of those who lived in a country or geographical region at the time when people of different cultures or ethnic groups arrived. The Lakota in the United States, the Mayas in Guatemala, and the Maori of New Zealand are all indigenous peoples. Most indigenous peoples have distinct social, cultural, economic, and political characteristics that are different from those of other people living the region. How do you think these communities are affected by globalization? What do you think globalization looks like from their point of view?

While they oppose globalization, many terrorists take advantage of the technology, transportation, and other advances that have been made possible by globalization. Terror groups frequently use the internet to promote their ideas and coordinate followers all over the world. Planes and other modes of transportation make it easy to travel and coordinate attacks in other countries.

What do you think? Is the world in danger of becoming too Americanized? If so, what can societies do to maintain their own cultures and traditions?

REINFORCING LOCAL CULTURES

In some ways, globalization can be a way to reinforce and strengthen local cultures. For example, technological advances in India give many people access to satellite television. While satellite TV can bring in broadcasts from other countries and cultures, it can also increase the number of regional channels available to the Indian people. Many of these regional channels broadcast Indian content. This gives viewers more opportunities to identify with local Indian culture.

Similarly, many multinational companies carefully consider the culture of the countries in which they do business, open offices, or sell products. For example, McDonald's creates regional menus in its restaurants that incorporate local tastes and customs. In Japan, there are seaweed-seasoned French fries. Samurai pork burgers are offered in Thailand. And in Taiwan, kids' meals come in reusable metal containers that are a local custom. Combining traditional customs with new global products is another way to reinforce and reaffirm local cultures.

A GLOBAL VILLAGE

In prior centuries, people were disconnected from other people and cultures. Because people were so separate and did not have a lot of interaction, they often felt little emotion for the challenges faced by others. For example, if an earthquake devastated China, destroying homes and killing large numbers of civilians, people in Europe were not greatly affected because they had no connection to China. They might not even know about the tragic event for days or weeks after it happened.

Today, globalization has connected people and cultures more closely than at any time in the past. Now, television news networks broadcast powerful images of famine, natural disasters, and war. By interviewing victims and showing the physical and emotional damage they experience, newscasters humanize an event occurring halfway around the world.

> Powerful images of human suffering on the internet, television, or in newspapers create emotional reactions in viewers.

Such emotional reactions can motivate people to take action. In some cases, public opinion can put significant pressure on governments to take action. In 1992, news coverage of the crisis in Somalia put pressure on U.S. government officials to intervene militarily to prevent a famine. And in 2017, the devastation caused by Hurricane Irma in the Caribbean inspired many people from countries around the world to donate money and supplies and to volunteer for relief efforts to aid the people affected by the storm.

BAND AID

In 1984, a British television documentary about famine in Ethiopia inspired a group of British musicians to organize a charity event to benefit the starving Ethiopian people. They called themselves Band Aid and recorded a song, "Do They Know It's Christmas?" and held a concert, raising nearly $15 million for famine relief efforts.

In 2014, musicians repeated the effort made by the original Band Aid and called themselves Band Aid 30, in honor of the event's 30-year anniversary.

You can listen to the original Band Aid recording at this site. How timely are these lyrics today?

 Band Aid song

The island of Saint Martin was hit hard by Hurricane Irma.

credit: Ministry of Defense, the Netherlands

CREATING GLOBAL VALUES

In some cases, globalization can do more than raise awareness and sympathy for people in need. It can also spread certain values related to issues of democracy, human rights, and health.

Some global institutions, including NGOs, multinational agencies, and government agencies, have promoted what they believe to be positive cultural values. These groups convey their ideas through mass communication, think tanks, education, and development projects. One organization, the International Campaign to Ban Landmines (ICBL), won the Nobel Peace Prize in 1997 in recognition for its work to organize global efforts to end the use of landmines.

Landmines are containers of explosive material that detonate when triggered by contact with a person or vehicle. They are designed to severely wound or kill a person or damage a vehicle with an explosive blast. These mines are generally buried within 6 inches of the earth's surface and are sometimes even laid above the ground. Most are placed by military groups during a conflict. Years after the conflict's end, many landmines remain active and dangerous.

> As a result, many civilians have
> been killed or seriously wounded
> after unknowingly straying into
> an unmarked minefield.

Jody Williams (1950–), the executive director of the ICBL, used the internet to spread information about the benefits of banning landmines. With a small staff and limited resources, Williams was able to build a global network of more than 1,100 groups for human rights, de-mining, and other humanitarian causes in more than 60 countries. These organizations worked around the world to ban landmines. Her work led to a significant international movement that shifted government attitudes toward the use of landmines.

PROTECTING LANGUAGES

As globalization has spread, so has the English language. Business, pop culture, entertainment, and more are dominated by English speakers. What might this mean for languages around the world? Some people fear the spread of English will mean the decline and eventual loss of some of the world's native languages.

TRUE NEWS

Linguists estimate that a language dies every two weeks.

Learn more about the loss of world languages and culture by reading this newspaper article. What is the connection between the environment and language? Why is biodiversity important both in nature and in culture?

 Loss Languages Guardian

In order to preserve language, some governments have imposed bans on what they determine to be a foreign intrusion of culture. In France, the French Academy routinely reviews for words from other languages, particularly English, and comes up with French equivalents. For example, "courriel" instead of "email." Even the word "hashtag," which is frequently used on Twitter and social media, was replaced with the French word "mot-dièse."

In China, the government is also attempting to remove foreign words. Authorities reviewed the brands and names of more than 20,000 Western companies and forced more than 2,000 of them to change to more Chinese-sounding names.

Because of globalization, people who were once isolated can communicate and connect with people who live thousands of miles away. These connections make it easier to exchange ideas, customs, and traditions and help people from different cultures better understand each other. At the same time, globalization can cause cultures to become more similar, which may result in the loss of customs. By understanding these risks, we can work together to preserve valuable cultures and traditions.

KEY QUESTIONS

- Who might see cultural globalization as a threat? Who might see it as a beneficial trend?
- Do you think a world in which everyone eats the same things, talks the same way, and consumes the same media would be a happy one? Why or why not?

PRESERVING CULTURE

As people share culture with one another, there is a danger that some pieces of a local culture will be lost and forgotten forever. What part of your life and culture do you want to save for future generations? What traditions are in danger of being forgotten and should be preserved?

- **Imagine that you are living one thousand years in the future.**

  - What do you think the people then will remember about today's world?

  - Do you think they will be able to understand what daily life was like?

  - What parts of our culture do you think will have survived?

  - What parts may not have survived? Why not?

- **Help a person living in the future better understand today's life, culture, and traditions.** Come up with a package filled with artifacts from your own life—objects, images, videos, recordings, documents, or other items. What will you include? Explain why you chose each item and its cultural significance.

> **To investigate more,** consider that many local communities have a historic preservation board or committee. Find out what artifacts are being considered for preservation or issues that are being debated by the board. Choose an issue or artifact to investigate and create arguments either for or against preserving the artifact.

VOCAB LAB

Write down what you think each word means. What root words can you find to help you? What does the context of the word tell you?

indigenous, **humanize**, **popular culture**, **stereotype**, **terrorism**, **traditions**, and **Westernization**.

Compare your definitions with those of your friends or classmates. Did you all come up with the same meanings? Turn to the text and glossary if you need help.

LANGUAGE AND CULTURE

Currently, the United States has no official language. Federal legislators have proposed laws to make English the country's official language, but no legislation has been passed to date.

- **Using the internet and other sources, research state and national debates on making English an official language.** You can start with the following articles.

  - "States where English is the official language"

     English official language WaPo

  - "Do You Speak American?"

     official American PBS

- **As you learn more about the issue, consider the following questions.**

  - What are the benefits and drawbacks of having an official language?

  - If there was such a law, what effect would it have on you, your community, your state, and the country?

  - What does the debate about a national language reveal about American society and culture?

  - Why do you think the United States does not have an official language?

- **Now think about the issue from the perspective of another country.** Many countries around the world have declared a national language. Choose a country to research and consider the following.

  - Does this country have an official language?

  - What other languages are spoken or used in the country?

  - How is globalization affecting the country's language(s)? How does this impact its culture?

  - What steps has the country taken or not taken to protect its language? How effective have these measures been?

- **Take a side and write a persuasive essay about whether or not a country should declare an official language.** Be sure to discuss the importance of language to a culture and the impact of globalization on language. Does declaring an official language have an effect on globalization and the future of language?

> **To investigate more,** consider the question, why should we study languages in school? Create a PowerPoint presentation that explains how language, culture, and globalization are connected.

VANISHING CULTURES

Many indigenous cultures are facing a battle between traditional ways of life and globalization. As older generations die out, many of the culture's traditions are dying with them.

- **Use the internet and other sources to research a specific indigenous culture.** You might choose the Maasai of Africa, the Wanniyala-Aetto of Sri Lanka, the Yanomami of South America, or another group of your choosing. Once you have chosen a group to investigate, consider the following.

  - Where does the group traditionally live? What are the climate and environment like?

  - What is their traditional lifestyle? How do they eat and gather food? What tools do they use to get and prepare food?

  - What ceremonies, celebrations, or festivals do they observe?

  - What role does the extended family play?

  - What types of jobs do people typically hold? How do they get around?

  - How are traditions passed from one generation to the next?

- **Next, research how globalization has impacted these indigenous people and their culture.** What changes have occurred in their environment, society, and political systems? What has caused these changes? How have these changes affected the group's culture, beliefs, and traditions? Prepare a presentation to share what you have learned with your class.

To investigate more, imagine that you were going to live with this group for a week. What items from your culture would you bring with you? Why are these items important to you? How would they help you to live with this indigenous group? What would people from this group think about the items you have brought? Write a diary entry to describe your visit.

Chapter 7

The Future of Globalization

What will the world be like 100 years from now?

It's not likely that globalization will go away. Instead, countries and individuals might become even more connected and dependent on each other as we work to solve some of the problems threatening our very existence.

• • • • • • • • • • • •

Globalization has changed the way we live. It has opened the door to new goods, ideas, and adventures. Advances in technology, communications, and transportation have made it possible to send people and products anywhere in the world. Globalization shows no sign of slowing down any time soon. In the years to come, globalization will bring a variety of new opportunities and challenges for people and nations around the world.

What kind of world can we look forward to in the future?

How will globalization continue to change our lives? We might never know the answers to these questions, but thinking about how we want the world to be in 10, 50, and even 100 years is a good way to make it happen!

AN INTEGRATED GLOBAL ECONOMY

Today, the global economy is more integrated than at any other time in history. According to a 2017 report by the OCP Policy Center, the global trade of goods and services included in the world GDP (gross domestic product) increased from less than 40 percent in 1990 to 60 percent today.[1] GDP is the total value of everything produced by all the people and companies in a country. In addition, the money flowing to developing countries as investments or for development has also increased.

Developing countries are playing more of a role in the global economy. Consider China, for example. Since 2009, China has been the world's largest exporter of goods. And since 2013, China has also become the world's largest trading nation, a position previously held by the United States. China's leap to become a global trading giant has happened incredibly quickly.

China exports many products, including electrical goods, data processing technologies, clothing and other textiles, and optical and medical equipment. China also exports a significant amount of raw materials, including steel. These raw materials are sold to other countries, where they are processed and used in products.

China's main trading partners are its neighbors—Hong Kong, South Korea, and Japan. China also conducts a large amount of trade with the United States and Germany. The rise of developing countries such as China in the global economy is expected to continue for years to come.

CHINA'S HISTORY

Throughout its long history, China traditionally followed more protectionist and isolationist trading policies. It avoided trading with other countries as much as possible. However, after the death of China's leader Mao Zedong (1893–1976), the country began to focus more on trade and foreign investment.

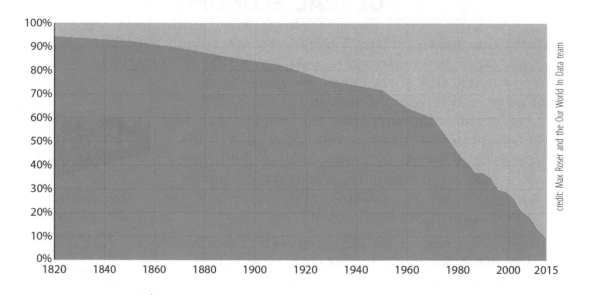

World population living in extreme poverty, 1820 to 2015

Share of people living in extreme poverty   Share of people not in extreme poverty

credit: Max Roser and the Our World In Data team

As developing countries participate more in the global economy, they can improve their own local economies and reduce poverty. In 1990, the number of absolute poor, defined as people who are unable to obtain adequate nutrition and shelter, was 1.85 billion worldwide. According to the World Bank, by 2013 the number of absolute poor dropped to 767 million.

TRUE NEWS

The decline in employment experienced by the United States during the 2008 recession was greater than that of any recession in recent decades.

AFFECTING THE WORLD: 2008 RECESSION

When countries are interconnected in a global economy, events in one country affect another, like dominoes falling in a row. In 2007–2008, the United States experienced the worst financial crisis since the Great Depression of the 1930s. The crisis began in 2007, when elevated U.S. home prices began to drop. The effects spread quickly through the entire U.S. financial industry.

The damage was not limited to banks and financial companies. Businesses that relied on loans and credit to conduct business also suffered. Banks stopped making the loans that most companies need to manage the flow of cash and do its work. The American car industry teetered on the brink of collapse. And stock prices dropped significantly. The country entered a deep recession, which is a drop in economic growth that lasts at least six months.

The U.S. recession had a ripple effect around the world. Other countries experienced similar financial crises. Japan and China suffered as the recession in the United States and Europe deeply cut demand for their products. Other less-developed countries could not sell as many goods and services abroad. Foreign investment in developing countries, which depend on this investment money to pay for new factories, roads, and equipment, also slowed.

Most of the world's major economies entered into recession. According to a World Bank 2009 report, almost no country was able to escape some impact from the financial crisis. In the future, similar economic swings that start in one country will have the potential to impact economies worldwide.

MIGRATION

Globalization has made it easier for people to move. People migrate to other countries for several reasons. In some cases, they travel to another country to find a job. Some countries might have a booming job market with many good-paying positions, while in other countries people struggle to find decent-paying work. In these cases, workers often leave their home country to find better jobs and lifestyles.

WHAT IS ECONOMIC DEVELOPMENT?

International investors often classify countries based on their level of economic development. Industrialized nations are sometimes called more economically developed countries (MEDCs), while less industrialized nations are called less economically developed countries (LEDCs).

Most people in MEDCs enjoy a higher standard of living. They have access to good education, healthcare, and employment opportunities. Most MEDCs also have secondary industries such as manufactured goods, banking, and insurance. People in MEDCs often live in towns and cities instead of the country. According to the UN, the United States, Canada, Japan, Australia, New Zealand, and all the countries in Europe are MEDCs.

TRUE NEWS

According to the UN, in 2015, 244 million people, or 3.3 percent of the world's population, lived outside their country of origin.

On the Move

Internal migration—or movement from one part of a country to another—is also increasing. People move to places with more resources, services, and opportunities, or to escape violence or natural disasters. The movement of people from rural areas to urban areas has led to the growth of cities worldwide.

For example, many graduates from Indian universities have difficulty finding good jobs in their home country. Some move to the United States, where their skills appeal to high-tech companies. Low-skilled laborers from Latin America have also left home due to lack of jobs or low wages and moved to the United States to take jobs in the growing service industry.

People also move to escape from areas in crisis. Millions of people have fled their countries to escape conflict, persecution, violence, or human rights violations. Some of these people are considered refugees because they can no longer live safely in their home countries.

In recent years, many refugees have come from Syria, Afghanistan, and South Sudan. In the Syrian civil war that began in 2011, the Syrian people have endured extreme violence as government forces and rebel groups have fought for control of the country. The fighting has caused tens of thousands of deaths as well as numerous human rights atrocities, including the alleged use of chemical weapons and torture. Millions of Syrians have fled the country looking for safety elsewhere, primarily in Europe.

IMMIGRATION BACKLASH

While many people welcome the flow of goods and money across borders, they have been less welcoming to the flow of people. Many countries are increasingly resistant to the mass migration brought about by conflicts around the globe or by people seeking better opportunities. They question the effects immigration will have on their country's culture and national identity.

A young refugee in a refugee camp in Bangladesh

credit: John Owens, VOA

Fear and distrust of people who are "different" cause some citizens to link immigration to social problems, such as unemployment and crime. According to a World Bank report, many countries strongly oppose liberal immigration and migration policies. Many maintain extensive legal barriers to prevent immigrants from seeking work or establishing a home inside their countries. Increasingly, immigration policies are becoming stricter as countries attempt to minimize the economic, cultural, and security effects of large movements of people across their borders.

In 2015, more than 1 million migrants and refugees arrived in Europe. This mass migration of people caused some governments in Europe to announce plans to adjust policies and strengthen borders to limit future mass migrations.

In Slovenia, the country's president granted the parliament the power to close the country's borders if necessary, due to a threat caused by migrations. In the United Kingdom, the government announced plans to halt a program to resettle refugee children.

TRUE NEWS

According to the UN, at the end of 2016, about 65.6 million people around the world were forced from their homes by conflict and persecution.

The immigration crisis is a good example of how globalization creates both opportunity for improvement in the world and also problems that need to be dealt with humanely and economically. In this article, read more about some of the issues related to immigration in today's world. Can you think of any solutions?

 Pew immigrants 2015

In the United States, anti-immigration sentiment has also grown. Donald Trump won the 2016 presidential election, while promising sweeping immigration reforms to limit the number of people coming into the country as well as deporting undocumented immigrants already in the country.

Shortly after taking office, citing national security, President Trump announced an executive order to temporarily ban travel to the United States by refugees and immigrants from some Muslim-majority countries. This travel ban has been challenged repeatedly in court. The future of immigration to the United States is still hazy, but the country's reputation as a safe haven has dissolved.

What has caused countries such as the United States and those in Europe to become less welcoming to immigrants?

Some countries claim they are not equipped to deal with the costs of supporting unemployed citizens of another nation. Others argue that immigrant workers are taking jobs and resources away from their own citizens.

These attitudes persist even as studies show that most immigrants are eager to work and are willing to take on jobs that citizens don't want, such as migrant farming. In addition, language and cultural differences can intensify the fear and distrust of immigrants that some people feel.

Despite these difficulties, most experts predict global migration will continue to rise in the coming years. Globalization has made it easier for people to find a safe place to live where they can find jobs and an improved standard of living.

U.S. Secretary of State John Kerry signs the Paris Agreement in April 2016, holding his granddaughter on his lap.

credit: U.S. Department of State

ENVIRONMENTAL CHALLENGES

Imagine what the planet was like 400 years ago. There were far more wild, natural areas, oceans and lakes were cleaner, and the air quality in most places was healthier. This was before industry took on such a large role in our lives.

As global connections, trade, and development have increased, valuable habitats and rainforests have been cleared to make way for roads, housing developments, farmland, and other projects. As factory output increases, so does the amount of carbon dioxide and other pollutants released into the air, water, and soil.

While many nations have put regulations in place to protect the environment, these laws vary from country to county. Instead of obeying a regulation, multinational corporations can simply move their operations to a country with fewer regulations. Although this may lead to higher profits for the corporation, it often leads to environmental damage in the host country.

TRUE NEWS

The increase in carbon dioxide emissions from industrialization is a leading factor in global warming.

What role will innovation play in the protection of the environment from global industry? Listen to a talk by UN Secretary-General António Guterres. How is the world going to solve the looming problem of climate change and inequality?

 2017 Web Summit Guterres

Although the United States originally approved the Paris Agreement, President Donald Trump announced in June 2017 that the United States planned to withdraw from it. The move drew much criticism from people and environmental groups within the United States and around the world. President Trump stated that the United States would be open to re-entering the Paris Agreement or a new treaty under terms that were more beneficial to American businesses and taxpayers. Do you agree or disagree with this approach?

The Paris Agreement sets a specific goal of keeping global temperatures from rising 2 degrees Celsius (3.6 degrees Fahrenheit).

• • • • • • • • • • • •

At the same time, globalization's advances in technology and communication have made it easier to fight environmental damage. Environmental groups can use the internet to more easily identify and alert people around the world about environmental damage and the companies that cause it. They can organize protests, boycotts, and other actions against the companies.

Global connections also make it easier for countries to band together in international agreements to protect the environment.

For example, many world leaders have met to discuss efforts to reduce the pollution that impacts climate change. In December 2015, the UN adopted the Paris Agreement to address climate change. The agreement, which took effect in November 2016, seeks to prevent increases in global temperatures by gradually reducing emissions of greenhouse gases. Throughout the years, the protection of the global environment has been a complex issue and is expected to present more challenges to the global community in the future.

BECOMING A GLOBAL CITIZEN

Through globalization, the world is becoming more connected every day. We are all global citizens. So what can we do today to be better citizens of the world?

- **Get informed**. Learn about the issues facing the world and globalization. Reading this book is one step, but there's so much more you can do. Read about current events and globalization in newspapers and other reputable media sources. Learn about new cultures or try learning a new language.

- **Share your story**. What is your family's immigration story? When did your family arrive in the United States? Share your story with others to help them understand the influences that brought you to where you are today.

- **Share your culture with others**. Share information about your culture—its language, food, and traditions—to help others learn about it. Establish relationships with people from other cultures and learn about their traditions and customs. By learning about our differences, we can better see the similarities.

- **Make yourself available**. Is there a new student in school from another country or culture? Reach out and help that person with the transition to their new environment. You might just develop a new friendship in the process.

Everyone can be a global citizen. By understanding the forces of globalization and learning about each other, we can begin to see beyond national borders. Globalization affects almost every part of our daily lives in ways that continue to evolve. Every day, we eat, shop, use products, and connect with people from around the world. It is an exciting time in the world's history. As global citizens working together to make the world a better place for all, we can create a solid foundation of global connections for years and generations to come.

KEY QUESTIONS

- What globalization issue interests you the most? The environment, immigration, trade? Why do you find this topic compelling?

- What are your ideas for solving immigration disputes in your country? Is there one solution that will make everyone safe and happy?

THINK GLOBALLY, ACT LOCALLY

Think globally, act locally is a principle that everyone can apply. It asks everyone, from governments and businesses to students and citizens, to consider the global impact of their actions.

- **What does it mean to think globally, act locally?** What are some specific examples of how this principle can be applied by:

  - Cities
  - Companies
  - Individuals

- **Identify and research a person or organization in your community that thinks globally and acts locally.** Write a profile of your subject, including specific examples about how they think globally and act locally. Consider the following.

  - What global concerns do they address in their work?

  - In what ways are they thinking about the global community?

  - What actions are they taking locally? How do their actions affect the local community?

  - How do both the global and local communities benefit?

To investigate more, find an example of a person or organization that is not living by the think global, act local principle. How do the subject's actions not align with this principle? How does that affect the global community? How does it affect the local community? What changes would the subject need to make to think globally and act locally?

VOCAB LAB 📖

Write down what you think each word means. What root words can you find to help you? What does the context of the word tell you?

boycott, **climate change**, **developing country**, **global warming**, **gross domestic product**, **immigrant**, **isolationism**, **migrate**, **persecution**, **recession**, **refugee**, and **secondary industry**.

Compare your definitions with those of your friends or classmates. Did you all come up with the same meanings? Turn to the text and glossary if you need help.

BE A GLOBAL CITIZEN

We are all global citizens. No matter where you live, you can get involved and make a difference in the world. Think about some issues facing the global community today. Poverty, refugees, hunger, environment, fair wages, healthcare, and education are just a few examples. What issue is most important to you?

- **Research some examples of local community service that are connected to your global issue.** Who has done work in your community to address this issue? What have they done and how has it impacted the local community?

- **Brainstorm ideas for your own volunteer or community-service project that addresses your area of global concern.** You might volunteer for an organization or create your own community-based project.

- **Fill out the details of your project: who, where, what, why, when, and how?** Recruit volunteers as needed. Develop a timeline or schedule to help everyone complete the project. Then go out and make a difference!

- **After you have completed the service project, create a presentation to share with your class.**

To investigate more, how does your service project fit into the principle of thinking globally, acting locally?

GLOSSARY

abroad: in or to a foreign country or countries.

acquit: to find someone not guilty of a criminal charge.

adapt: to become used to new conditions or to make something suitable for a new use.

advocate: to recommend or support publically.

advocacy: public support for or recommendation of a particular cause or policy.

ally: a partner in an alliance.

altitude: height above sea level.

amend: to change.

Americanization: the influence of American businesses and culture on foreign people and countries.

apartheid: a policy or system of segregation or discrimination on grounds of race.

arbitration: the process where someone settles a dispute between other people.

authority: the power or right to give orders, make decisions, and enforce obedience.

bankruptcy: a legal proceeding involving a person or business that is unable to repay outstanding debts.

barter: to trade by exchanging one good or service for another.

BCE: put after a date, BCE stands for Before Common Era and counts years down to zero. CE stands for Common Era and counts years up from zero. This book was published in 2018 CE.

beneficial: favorable or advantageous.

bilateral: involving two parties such as countries.

binding: an agreement that cannot be legally broken.

biodiversity: the range of living things in an area.

black market: illegal trade in goods that are scarce.

border: a line separating two political or geographical areas, especially countries.

boycott: refusing to buy or sell goods as part of a protest.

brand: a type of product manufactured by a particular company under a particular name.

Brexit: the potential withdrawal of the United Kingdom from the European Union.

budget: a plan for how money will be spent.

capital: money used to start or expand a business.

capitalism: an economic and political system in which a country's trade and industry are controlled by private owners for profit, rather than by the state.

caravan: a group of travelers and pack animals on a journey.

carbon dioxide: a gas formed by the burning of fossil fuels, the rotting of plants and animals, and the breathing out of animals or humans.

charter: a written document by which an institution such as a company, NGO, college, or city is created and its rights and privileges defined.

chemical: the pure form of a substance. Some chemicals can be combined or broken up to create new chemicals.

citizen: a person who legally belongs to a country and has the rights and protection of that country.

climate: the weather patterns in an area during a long period of time.

climate change: changes to the average weather patterns in an area during a long period of time.

collaboration: working with others.

collective action: when a group of people work together to solve a problem.

colony: a country or area that is under the political control of another country.

combustion engine: an engine that runs on heat, either from a furnace or from inside the engine itself.

common market: a group of countries imposing few or no duties on trade with one another and a common tariff on trade with other countries.

communism: an economic and political system in which the government owns everything used in the production and distribution of goods.

community: a group of people who live in the same place or who share key characteristics such as religion or language.

comparative advantage: the ability of an individual or group to carry out a particular economic activity (such as making a specific product) more efficiently than another activity.

conflict: a fight or strong disagreement.

consensus: a general agreement.

conservation: to use something carefully, so it doesn't get used up.

constitution: a document containing the basic laws and beliefs of a country.

consumer: a person who buys goods and services.

continent: one of Earth's largest land areas.

controversy: an argument that involves many people who strongly disagree.

copyright protection: laws that protect original works of authorship, including literary, dramatic, musical, and artistic works, such as poetry, novels, movies, songs, computer software, and architecture.

corrupt: to act dishonestly in return for money or personal gain.

culture: the beliefs and way of life of a group of people.

currency: the system of money produced by a government in a country.

customary: according to the customs or usual practices associated with a particular society.

customs: traditions or ways of doing things, including dress, food, and holidays. Also the government agency that collects taxes on imports and exports.

deficit: a shortage of something.

democracy: a form of government in which all people can vote for representatives.

demographic: a group of people who share the same qualities, such as age or gender.

developing country: a poor country that is trying to become more advanced.

diplomacy: managing international relations, typically by a country's representatives abroad.

diplomat: a person sent by the government to deal with another country.

diplomatic immunity: the exemption from certain laws and taxes granted to diplomats by the country in which they are working.

discrimination: the unjust or prejudicial treatment of different categories of people or things, especially on the grounds of race, age, or sex.

displaced: forced from one's home due to war or natural disaster.

dispute: a disagreement, argument, or debate.

diversify: to vary or enlarge the number of different objects, people, or places of operation.

domestic: within a home country.

dominant: stronger or more controlling than another.

duty: a type of tax often placed on imports and exports.

e-commerce: business conducted electronically on the internet.

economy: a system of producing and consuming goods and services.

efficiency: the ability to do or make something well and without waste.

embargo: an official ban on trade or other commercial activity with a particular country.

emerging economy: a country that has some characteristics of a developed market, but does not meet standards to be a developed market.

emissions: something sent or given off, such as smoke, gas, heat, or light.

empathy: the ability to share the feelings of others.

empire: a group of states or countries under a single supreme authority, especially an emperor or empress.

encroach: to intrude on a person's territory or rights.

enforce: to carry out a law.

enterprise: a business or company.

environment: a natural area with animals, plants, rocks, soil, and water.

estimate: to make an educated guess.

GLOSSARY

ethnic: related to a group with a common national or cultural tradition.

euro: the official currency of the European Union.

European Coal and Steel Community (ECSC): an organization of six European countries set up after World War II to regulate their industrial production under a centralized authority.

European Economic Community (EEC): an economic union of member states in Europe that evolved into the EU.

European Union (EU): a political and economic union of 28 members, mostly in Europe.

exchange rate: the difference in value between money in one country and money in another country.

exploit: to benefit unfairly from someone else's work.

export: any good or service that is shipped outside the country or brings in money from other countries.

famine: a period of great hunger and lack of food for a large population.

forum: a place where ideas and views on a particular issue can be exchanged.

franchise: an authorization granted by a government or company to an individual or group enabling them to carry out specified commercial activities.

free-market economy: a system where people are free to buy and sell things they own.

fundamental: a central or primary rule or principle on which something is based.

GATT (General Agreement on Trade and Tariffs): a legal agreement between many countries whose overall purpose was to promote international trade by reducing or eliminating trade barriers such as tariffs or quotas.

Geneva Conventions: rules that apply in times of armed conflict and seek to protect people who are not or are no longer taking part in hostilities.

genocide: the deliberate killing of a large group of people based on race, ethnicity, or nationality.

global: relating to the entire world.

global positioning system (GPS): a system of satellites, computers, and receivers that determines the location of a receiver on Earth. This is done by calculating the time difference for signals from different satellites to reach the receiver.

globalization: the integration of the world economy through trade, money, and labor.

global warming: a gradual increase in the overall temperature of the earth's atmosphere.

goods: things to use or sell.

Great Depression: the economic turndown that began with the stock market crash in 1929 and continued through the 1930s.

greenhouse gas: a gas in the atmosphere that traps the sun's heat.

gross domestic product (GDP): the total value of goods produced and services provided in a country during one year.

habitat: the natural area where a plant or an animal lives.

haven: a place where a person is protected from danger.

human rights: the rights that belong to all people, such as freedom from torture, the right to live, and freedom from slavery.

humanitarian aid: aid provided typically in response to crises such as natural disasters and war.

humanize: to give something a human character.

immigrant: a person who comes to settle in a new country.

immigration: moving to a new country to live there.

import: any good or service that is brought in from another country.

indigenous: native to a place.

industrialized: a country with a lot of manufacturing.

inequality: differences in opportunity and treatment based on social, ethnic, racial, or economic qualities.

infrastructure: the basic physical and organizational structures and facilities of a society.

integrate: to become part of.

intellectual property: property that comes from the work of the mind.

interconnected: when two or more things have an impact on each other.

interdependent: two or more people or things dependent on each other.

intergovernmental: relating to or conducted between two or more governments.

international: involving two or more countries.

International Criminal Court (ICC): an international court that has the authority to prosecute individuals for the crimes of genocide, crimes against humanity, and war crimes.

International Court of Justice (ICJ): an international court that settles disputes between countries and advises the various bodies of the United Nations.

investor: a person who gives a company money in exchange for future profits.

isolationism: the policy of remaining apart from other countries and not getting involved in their affairs.

judicial: the branch of government consisting of courts with judges who decide if laws have been broken.

jurisdiction: the official power to make legal decisions and judgments.

justice: fair action or treatment based on the law.

labor: work, or people who do work.

LEDC: less economically developed country.

legislation: laws.

legislature: a government body that creates laws.

legitimate: following the laws or rules.

lobbyist: a person who tries to influence legislators on behalf of a special interest, business, or cause.

logo: a symbol used to identify a company that appears on its products and in its marketing.

manufacturing: to make large quantities of products in factories using machines.

Maastricht Treaty: a treaty signed by the leaders of 12 European nations that stated their intentions to create a common economic and monetary union.

manga: comics created in Japan or in the Japanese language.

mass migration: the migration of large groups of people from one area to another.

MEDC: more economically developed country.

mediator: a person who attempts to make people involved in a conflict come to an agreement.

Middle Ages: the period of European history after the fall of the Roman Empire, from about 350 to 1450 CE.

migrant: a person who moves from place to place to find work.

migrate: to move from one region to another.

militia: an army made up of citizens instead of professional soldiers.

minimum wage: the lowest hourly wage allowed to be paid by law.

merchant: a person who buys and sells goods for a profit.

migrate: to move from one place to another.

monetary system: the system used by a country to provide money and to control the exchange of money.

monopoly: the exclusive possession or control of the supply or trade in a commodity or service.

multilateral: agreed upon or participated in by three or more parties, especially the governments of different countries.

multinational: including or involving several countries or individuals of several nationalities.

national identity: the cultures, traditions, language, and politics of a country.

nationality: the status of belonging to a particular nation.

natural resource: something found in nature that is useful to humans, such as water to drink, trees to burn, and fish to eat.

negotiation: working to reach an agreement, compromise, or treaty through bargaining and discussing.

network: a group or system of interconnected people or things.

neutral: not favoring one side over another.

nongovernmental organization (NGO): a nonprofit set up by ordinary people, usually to help people or the environment.

GLOSSARY

North American Free Trade Agreement (NAFTA): a treaty between Canada, Mexico, and the United States.

notorious: famous or well-known, particularly for a negative act or quality.

Nuclear Non-Proliferation Treaty (NPT): an international treaty whose objective is to prevent the spread of nuclear weapons and weapons technology.

nuclear: energy produced when the nucleus of an atom is split apart.

Paris Agreement: an agreement within the United Nations Framework Convention on Climate Change that deals with the reduction of greenhouse gas emissions.

persecution: hostility and ill-treatment, often because of race, religion, or nationality.

perspective: a person's point of view.

petroleum: a non-renewable fossil fuel used to heat homes and fuel cars. Also called oil or gasoline.

politics: the business of governments.

popular culture: books, movies, music, and other forms of art that appear to large populations of people.

pre-emptive: something done to prevent a future action, especially an attack.

price-setting: determining the amount of money to charge for goods or services.

productivity: the quality of working hard and getting good results, having the power to produce.

profit: financial gain, income less expenses.

proportional: corresponding in size or amount to something else.

prosecute: to institute legal proceedings against a person or organization.

prosperity: the condition of being successful.

protectionism: the practice of shielding a country's domestic industries from foreign competition by taxing imports.

prototype: a working model or mock-up that allows engineers to test their solution.

provision: the action of providing or supplying something for use.

quantity: the amount of something.

quota: a limit on the quantity of a specific imported good.

ratify: to approve formally.

recession: a temporary economic slowdown.

reciprocity: the practice of exchanging things with others for mutual benefit. Also responding to a gesture or action by making a corresponding one.

referendum: an occasion when everyone in a country can vote to make a decision about something.

refugee: someone escaping war, persecution, or natural disaster.

regulation: an official rule or law.

resources: the wealth of a country or its means of producing wealth.

retaliate: to fight back.

replica: an exact copy or model.

reputable: generally considered to be honest and reliable.

revenue: income.

revolutionize: to transform, or make a huge and complete change.

sanction: a penalty for disobeying a law or rule.

sanitation: conditions relating to public health, especially the provision of clean drinking water and adequate sewage disposal.

satellite communication system: a system that uses satellites to relay and amplify radio telecommunications signals.

scarce: when there isn't enough of something.

secondary industry: an industry that converts the raw materials provided by primary industry into products for the consumer, such as a manufacturing industry.

secretary-general: the leader of the United Nations.

self-determination: the process by which a country determines its own statehood and forms its own allegiances and government.

Silk Road: the ancient network of trade routes connecting the Mediterranean Sea and China by land.

slogan: a short and memorable phrase used in advertising.

sovereign: having supreme or ultimate power.

specialization: the process of concentrating on and becoming expert in a particular subject or skill.

sponsorship: giving money or support.

stable: reliable and steady, not likely to change.

standard of living: the degree of wealth and material comfort available to a person or community.

steam engine: an engine powered by steam, first invented by James Watt in 1775.

stereotype: to make a judgment about a group of individuals.

subsidy: a sum of money granted by the government or a public body to assist an industry or business.

superpower: a very powerful and influential nation, used especially with reference to the United States and the former Soviet Union.

supply and demand: the rule that prices go up and down depending on how much there is of something and how much people want it.

supranational: having power or influence that transcends national boundaries or governments.

surplus: more than what is needed.

sustainable: a process or resource that can be used without being completely used up or destroyed.

systematic: done or acting according to a fixed plan or system.

tariff: taxes, duties, or charges imposed by a government on imports or exports.

tax: an extra charge put on a product by the government. The government gets the extra money.

technology: the tools, methods, and systems used to solve a problem or do work.

textile: having to do with cloth or fabric.

trade: buying and selling goods and services.

trade agreement: an agreement the regulates trade, tariffs, and other trade restrictions between two or more countries.

trade barrier: government restrictions on international trade.

trade deficit: when a country imports more goods and services than it exports.

trade imbalance: when a country's imports and exports are not equal.

trade regulation: a law that governs trade.

trade restriction: a barrier to the trade between two countries, such a tariffs, quotas, subsidies, and embargos.

trade surplus: when a country exports more goods and services than it imports.

tradition: a custom or belief that has been handed down in a community or culture through many years.

transnational corporation: a corporate organization that owns or controls production of goods or services in two or more countries other than its home country.

treaty: a formal agreement among countries.

tribunal: a court of justice.

unemployment: joblessness.

United Nations (UN): an international organization created to promote peace and cooperation among nations.

value: how much money something is worth. Also a strongly held belief about what is valuable, important, or acceptable.

veto: to reject a law or policy.

violate: to break or fail to comply with a rule or agreement.

vulnerable: susceptible to physical or emotional attack or harm.

weapons of mass destruction: weapons capable of causing widespread death and destruction.

Westernization: the influence of culture from the United States and Western Europe on other countries and cultures around the world.

World Trade Organization (WTO): an intergovernmental organization that regulates international trade.

RESOURCES

BOOKS

Bernstein, William J. *A Splendid Exchange: How Trade Shaped the World.* Atlantic Monthly Press, 2008.

Haugen, David, and Rachael Mach. *Globalization (Opposing Viewpoints).* Greenhaven Press, 2010.

Heing, Bridey. *Critical Perspectives on Free Trade and Globalization (Analyzing the Issues).* Enslow, 2018.

Idzikowski, Lisa. *Globalization and Free Trade (Introducing Issues With Opposing Viewpoints).* Greenhaven Press, 2018.

Mann, Charles C., and Rebecca Stefoff. *1493 for Young People: From Columbus's Voyage to Globalization (For Young People Series).* Triangle Square, 2016.

Rothstein, Jeffrey S. *When Good Jobs Go Bad: Globalization, De-unionization, and Declining Job Quality in the North American Auto Industry.* Rutgers University Press, 2016.

Steger, Manfred B. *Globalization: A Very Short Introduction.* Oxford University Press, 2017.

SOURCE NOTES

INTRODUCTION

1 rollingstone.com/music/news/pitbulls-we-are-one-ole-ola-selected-as-official-world-cup-song-20140124

2 un.org/en/sections/member-states/growth-united-nations-membership-1945-present/index.html

3 polgeonow.com/2011/04/how-many-countries-are-there-in-world.html

CHAPTER 1

1 thocp.net/companies/att/att_company.htm

2 usatoday.com/story/travel/roadwarriorvoices/2016/01/10/this-is-what-it-was-like-to-fly-in-the-1930s/83283086

3 credit-suisse.com/us/en/about-us/research/research-institute/news-and-videos/articles/news-and-expertise/2016/11/en/the-global-wealth-report-2016.html

CHAPTER 2

1 eia.gov/tools/faqs/faq.php?id=727&t=6

2 thebalance.com/u-s-imports-and-exports-components-and-statistics-3306270

3 thebalance.com/u-s-trade-deficit-causes-effects-trade-partners-3306276

CHAPTER 3

1 corporate.walmart.com/our-story

CHAPTER 6

1 blogs.voanews.com/all-about-america/2015/05/18/top-10-most-popular-ethnic-cuisines-in-us

CHAPTER 7

1 ocppc.ma/sites/default/files/OCPPC-PB1718.pdf

QR CODE GLOSSARY

page 5: youtube.com/watch?v=PoD8SCoL-2Q

page 15: atlantic-cable.com/Cables/1956TAT-1/TAT-1-Opening.mp3

page 16: ted.com/talks/tim_berners_lee_on_the_next_web

page 28: youtube.com/watch?v=NI9TLDIPVcs

page 34: nytimes.com/2013/04/25/world/asia/bangladesh-building-collapse.html

page 34: nytimes.com/2012/12/07/world/asia/bangladesh-fire-exposes-safety-gap-in-supply-chain.html

page 34: nytimes.com/2013/05/02/business/some-retailers-rethink-their-role-in-bangladesh.html

page 42: youtube.com/watch?v=B3u4EFTwprM

page 43: vault.sierraclub.org/trade/downloads/nafta-and-mexico.pdf

page 44: economist.com/content/big-mac-index

page 46: nytimes.com/2016/09/29/business/economy/more-wealth-more-jobs-but-not-for-everyone-what-fuels-the-backlash-on-trade.html?mtrref=undefined&_r=0

page 46: cbsnews.com/news/the-toughest-question-about-global-trade

page 55: eur-lex.europa.eu/legal-content/EN/TXT/?uri=CELEX:12012P/TXT

page 58: azdailysun.com/news/local/community/tuba-city-doctor-reflects-on-doctors-without-borders-trip/article_9cde99b0-c5c5-5ca3-9988-f5d17b4c7ebf.html

page 62: ecb.europa.eu/press/pr/date/1998/html/pr981231_2.en.html

page 68: youtube.com/watch?v=zpM-nkhZCgk&t=336s

page 70: youtube.com/watch?v=MZFUuGOPLPg

page 70: un.org/en/universal-declaration-human-rights

page 78: ohchr.org/EN/ProfessionalInterest/Pages/CoreInstruments.aspx

page 85: pbs.org/newshour/bb/world-jan-june12-china_02-13

page 89: youtube.com/watch?v=bjQzJAKxTrE

page 91: theguardian.com/environment/2014/jun/08/why-we-are-losing-a-world-of-languages

page 92: youtube.com/channel/UCmbtQpU9Hd-RtiDmdRbHoUw

page 94: washingtonpost.com/blogs/govbeat/wp/2014/08/12/states-where-english-is-the-official-language/?utm_term=.0dd8281e3e79

page 94: pbs.org/speak/seatosea/officialamerican

page 104: pewglobal.org/2016/08/02/number-of-refugees-to-europe-surges-to-record-1-3-million-in-2015

page 105: youtube.com/watch?v=WiE17YsV1Bw

INDEX

INDEX